Contents

Contributors

Oksana Antonenko is Senior Fellow for Russia and Eurasia at the IISS. She has facilitated meetings between Georgian and South Ossetian officials and experts with the aim of promoting conflict resolution in the Georgian–South Ossetian conflict.

Carl Bildt is Sweden's Minister for Foreign Affairs. He was Prime Minister of Sweden from 1991 to 1994. He has held a number of positions at the international level, including Special Envoy of the UN Secretary-General to the Balkans from 1999 to 2001. In 1996 and 1997, he was High Representative of the international community in Bosnia-Herzegovina. From 1995 to 1997, he was the European Union's Special Representative for the Former Yugoslavia and in 1995, European co-chair of the Dayton peace conference.

Dr John Chipman is Director-General and Chief Executive of the IISS. He conceived and launched the Shangri-La Dialogue, the annual forum for consultations between defence ministers, military chiefs and analysts in the Asia-Pacific, of which the seventh took place in 2008. In 2004 he transferred the concept to the Gulf with the convening in Bahrain of the Manama Dialogue, of which the fifth took place in 2008.

Sir Ronald Cohen is chairman of the Portland Trust, which works to encourage peace and stability between Palestinians and Israelis through economic development. He is a leading private-equity investor and a founder of the private-equity industry in Europe. He is co-founder of private-equity firm Apax Partners and Chairman of Portland Capital, an investment-management firm.

Lieutenant-General Karl Eikenberry is Deputy Chairman of NATO's Military Committee. Previously, he was Commander of the Combined Forces Command – Afghanistan. Among other strategic, policy and political–military posts, he has held the position of Director for Strategic Planning and Policy for US Pacific Command.

Dr Robert Gates has been United States Secretary of Defense since 2006, and is to remain in this post in the Obama administration. A career officer in the Central Intelligence Agency, he was Director of Central Intelligence from 1991 to 1993. Prior to this, he served as Assistant to President George H.W. Bush and as Deputy National Security Adviser.

William Hague is the United Kingdom's Shadow Foreign Secretary and Conservative Member of Parliament for Richmond, Yorkshire. He was leader of the Conservative Party between 1997 and 2001.

Han Seung-soo is Prime Minister of the Republic of Korea. He has been Korea's Minister of Foreign Affairs and its Ambassador to the United States. In 2001, he was elected President of the 56th Session of the United Nations General Assembly. In 2007, he was appointed by UN Secretary-General Ban Ki-moon as a Special Envoy on Climate Change.

Dr Tim Huxley is Executive Director of IISS-Asia, located in Singapore, and Editor of the *Adelphi* series. He joined the IISS in 2003, having previously been Reader in Southeast Asian Politics and Director of the Centre for Southeast Asian Studies at the University of Hull.

Nigel Inkster is Director of Transnational Threats and Political Risk at the IISS. From 1975 to 2006, he served in the British Secret Intelligence Service. He spent seven years on the board of SIS, the last two as Assistant Chief and Director for Operations and Intelligence. He has worked in Asia, Latin America and Europe.

Dr Jakob Kellenberger is President of the International Committee of the Red Cross. He was previously in Switzerland's diplomatic service, and was State Secretary for Foreign Affairs from 1992 to 1999.

Lee Hsien Loong is Prime Minister of Singapore. He has also served as Singapore's Finance Minister, Deputy Prime Minister and Chairman of the Monetary Authority of Singapore. Before entering politics, he served as an officer in the Singapore Armed Forces, attaining the rank of Brigadier-General.

Lieutenant-General Ma Xiaotian is Deputy Chief of Staff of the People's Liberation Army of the People's Republic of China, and a Lieutenant-General in the People's Liberation Army Air Force.

Dr Jeffrey Mazo is Managing Editor of *Survival*, the bimonthly journal of the IISS, and Assistant Editor of *Strategic Survey*, the

Institute's annual review of strategic affairs. He is currently researching the security and policy implications of climate change.

Michael McDevitt is Director of the Center for Strategic Studies at the Center for Naval Analyses. He served in the United States Navy, reaching the rank of Rear Admiral. He was Commandant of the National War College from 1995 to 1997.

Shiv Shankar Menon has been Indian Foreign Secretary since 2006. He has also served as India's High Commissioner to Pakistan, Ambassador to China, High Commissioner to Sri Lanka and Ambassador to Israel, among other diplomatic postings.

Alexander Nicoll is Director of Editorial at the IISS. He is the Editor of the Institute's publications *Strategic Survey* and *Strategic Comments*. He was previously a journalist at the *Financial Times* (*FT*), where he was Defence Correspondent from 1997 to 2002. He has also been the *FT*'s Asia Editor and Consulting Editor of the Indian newspaper *Business Standard*.

General Sir David Richards is Commander-in-Chief of Land Forces in the British Army. He is to take over as Chief of the General Staff in August 2009. Among the responsibilities he has held are command of the UK Contingent in East Timor in 1999 and command of the UK Joint Task Force in Sierra Leone in 2000. From 2006 to 2007, he served as Commander of the International Security Assistance Force in Afghanistan.

Francesc Vendrell is a Spanish diplomat. He was the EU Special Representative for Afghanistan from 2002 to 2008. Prior to this, he was Personal Representative of the UN Secretary-General for Afghanistan and Head of the United Nations Special Mission to Afghanistan. He has worked for the UN in the Caucasus, Papua New Guinea, Cambodia, East Timor and a number of Central American states, including Nicaragua and Cuba.

Note

The texts in this volume have been edited lightly in order to ensure clarity, but are as true as possible to the words spoken.

Foreword

The International Institute for Strategic Studies celebrated its 50th anniversary in 2008. Founded to promote broad, knowledgeable discussion of nuclear issues, the IISS has developed into a global body with a wide range of activities and offices in Washington and Singapore, as well as London. Impartial, fact-based, policy-relevant research remains at the core of the Institute's work, with a focus on traditional themes such as defence policy, military capabilities, nuclear proliferation and transatlantic relations, as well as region-specific programmes and newer topics such as the security ramifications of failed states and climate change. The Institute's publications – the *Adelphi* series, the annual *Military Balance* and *Strategic Survey*, the bimonthly *Survival* and monthly *Strategic Comments*, as well as the *Armed Conflict Database* and regular *Strategic Dossiers* – all reflect this work. The Institute has meanwhile created new mechanisms for international diplomacy, beginning with the annual Shangri-La Dialogue, which brings together defence ministers and military chiefs from the Asia-Pacific, and the Manama Dialogue, which performs a similar role in the Persian Gulf region. During 2008 the Institute initiated a new National Forum in New Delhi, and conducted high-level meetings in Seoul and Tokyo. This Adelphi Paper offers a selection of the speeches and papers from IISS events during 2008. We thank all those who have helped to animate IISS discussions during our 50th anniversary year.

Dr John Chipman CMG
Director-General and Chief Executive, IISS

Introduction

Alexander Nicoll and Tim Huxley

Like most years in the 50-year history of the International Institute for Strategic Studies, 2008 saw events that could have significant consequences for international relations and global balances of power. These included the election of Barack Obama, a liberal and America's first black president, who is likely to strike a different tone from that of his conservative, unilateralist predecessor George W. Bush. In addition, the brief war in Georgia caused the West to look at Russia with more watchful eyes; and a cataclysmic crisis in the world's financial markets seemed to threaten globalisation and even capitalism – and to herald a period of greater economic austerity. These were all important events. But even as they occurred, the risks and dangers that have been the core focus of the work of the IISS during the past half-century continued to hang over the world and to demand to be addressed through strategy and patient, complex effort.

Among these were, in particular, the threats arising from existing and future nuclear arsenals, anxiety over which provided the impetus for the Institute's founding in 1958. Concerns about nuclear proliferation continue to grow. Other persistent issues that require detailed study include the political tensions, differences and imbalances that underlie conflict; the manner in which warfare, including terrorism, is carried on; and the difficulties involved in resolving conflicts. The years since the Second World War have seen the development of international structures in Europe, but there is still constant debate about Europe's nature and future; meanwhile in Asia, an uneasy status quo has been in place since the wars in Korea and

Vietnam, relying heavily on the strong regional military presence of the United States. As China and India gain economic clout, and as America's international standing suffers from its adventure in Iraq, that status quo may change. In addition to these perennial questions affecting international security, world leaders are paying closer attention to a set of issues that are by no means new, but have risen higher on the political agenda: for example, how to cope with natural disasters, and how to ensure a future for the planet in the face of environmental dangers, including global warming. In the face of so many variables, it is small wonder that there have been efforts to develop the 'science' of assessing risk.

In its 50th anniversary year, the IISS held a large number of high-level conferences around the world. Speeches given at these events addressed all of these issues, and this Adelphi Paper offers a selection of them. The speakers were statesmen, senior military officers, high officials and international security experts. All were concerned first and foremost with the pressing issues of the moment, as their duties required them to be. But the fact that they addressed recurrent themes testifies to the enduring nature of the strategic challenges faced by policymakers. Just as the past year has seen significant events, so too, on a grander scale, has the entire half-century of the IISS's existence: the Cold War, the Vietnam War, the collapse of the Soviet Union and of communism, China's Cultural Revolution and the country's subsequent economic rise, the 2001 terrorist attacks on the United States, and so on. Yet the underlying threats and dilemmas that confront the modern world have persisted.

It is not only in the Institute's conferences that these issues are reflected. In the *Adelphi* series in 2008, the IISS published a paper on Iran, the country currently posing the greatest nuclear-proliferation challenge; a paper on how terrorist campaigns are brought to an end; a paper intended to stimulate debate on how nuclear weapons might be abolished; a paper studying the record of the United Nations Security Council in dealing with conflicts; and a paper on Europe's efforts to improve its crisis-management capabilities. The IISS publications *Strategic Survey*, *Survival* and *Strategic Comments*, even as they analyse recent events, continually explore the enduring themes that provide the backbone of the Institute's work.

Sir Michael Howard, the British historian and a founder of the IISS, has said that those who established the Institute in 1958:

> Never had the audacity to claim to tell people what to think about strategic affairs, much less what to do about them. Our hope was simply to persuade people at least *to* think about

them; not only the military and political experts whose job it was, but everyone with a vote; and to provide them with accurate information so that they could think intelligently; possibly also to provide some guide to priorities, as to what was important, and what less so.

It is in this spirit of stimulating public debate on security issues that the Institute publishes this Adelphi Paper. Not only does it lend wider circulation to some of the important contributions to IISS conferences during the 50th anniversary year, but it provides a snapshot of global security challenges as viewed by the people seeking to cope with them in 2008. If this volume has an overall theme, it is one of enormous global change, accompanied by perennial challenges.

New thinking on nuclear weapons

In his address to the IISS's 50th anniversary dinner in London, Carl Bildt, Sweden's minister for foreign affairs, remarked that 'to say that much has changed during this half-century is certainly not an exaggeration'. Fifty years previously, Sweden had planned to acquire nuclear weapons, some of the targets of which would have been the capitals of countries that are now members of the European Union and the North Atlantic Treaty Organisation. Bildt, who has been Sweden's prime minister and the European Union's special representative in the former Yugoslavia, said that a defining feature of our time had been 'the uniquely peaceful implosion of the Soviet empire'. Yet as Europe seeks to build a new order of peace and prosperity, 'we are all aware of the major strategic challenges confronting us'. Among these, Bildt identified climate change and nuclear proliferation as the two most difficult. Handling them, he said, 'will call for far-reaching changes to the structures of international cooperation'.

A striking feature of Western discourse on nuclear proliferation in 2008 has been the emergence of new thinking – even if this has not yet translated into progress in dealing with the principal pressing challenge, that from Iran. In this vein, the British Conservative politician William Hague set out a detailed set of proposals in an IISS address in London. Hague, a former leader of his party and currently its chief spokesman on foreign affairs, argued that the tendency to deal with each proliferation problem as a unique issue 'fundamentally hampers our ability to stem the global spread of nuclear weapons'. He called for new efforts to reverse what he saw as the decline of the Nuclear Non-Proliferation Treaty and, in particular, to orchestrate a concerted response when a country breaches the treaty or withdraws from it. Hague called for a strengthening of the International Atomic Energy Agency, better efforts to interdict trade in nuclear technology, and the disruption of financing for proliferators. He also believed there should be mechanisms to bring the nuclear fuel cycle under international control, such as partnerships between states producing nuclear fuel, or a network of fuel banks. This was a point made by Bildt as well, who said that 'a critically important political challenge in the next few years must be to develop multinational and internationally controlled facilities for handling sensitive parts of the nuclear fuel cycle'. The issue was also highlighted in 2008 by an IISS Strategic Dossier, *Nuclear Programmes in the Middle East: In the shadow of Iran*, which documented the plans of 13 countries in the greater Middle East to explore civilian nuclear energy.

The revival of the discussion on curbing nuclear weapons is partly due to four American statesmen, George Shultz, Henry Kissinger, William Perry and Sam Nunn, who argued in 2007 that the world should seek to rid itself of nuclear weapons because reliance on them for deterrence was 'becoming increasingly hazardous and decreasingly effective'.[1] Both Bildt and Hague felt that this was an argument that should, if accepted, produce a substantial reduction in American and Russian nuclear arsenals, which would in turn bolster efforts against proliferation in general. In an Adelphi Paper published in 2008, *Abolishing Nuclear Weapons*, George Perkovich and James Acton examined possible steps towards abolition, as well as the challenges of verification and of managing the civil nuclear industry so as to prevent rearmament.

The urgent need to revitalise counter-proliferation efforts is clearly an important theme of contemporary security discussions, but requires determined backing from the world's major powers to be set in motion. As a presidential candidate, Obama spoke on the need for cuts in nuclear arsenals and for a new approach in dealing with Iran. A 2008 Adelphi Paper by Mark Fitzpatrick, *The Iranian Nuclear Crisis: Avoiding worst-case outcomes*, argued that the risks of Iran achieving a nuclear-weapons capability and stimulating a 'proliferation cascade' in the Middle East were still best minimised by reinforcing the binary choice presented to Iran of cooperation or isolation, and by strengthening denial of supply of nuclear material and knowledge. However, Bildt was calling for something more: a reorganisation of the international institutions, including the United Nations, that deal with the nuclear issue. This would require

---

[1]   George P. Shultz, William J. Perry, Henry A. Kissinger and Sam Nunn, 'A World Free of Nuclear Weapons', *Wall Street Journal*, 4 January 2007.

much greater international impetus and consensus on this issue than has so far been evident. There is a risk that the only stimulus sufficient to provoke this would be the shock of Iran actually acquiring a nuclear weapon. By that time, it could be too late for any reinforcement of international institutions to have any meaningful effect, because many other countries would be likely to seek to acquire nuclear weapons, and few would wish to dispense with them.

Persistent conflicts, inadequate capabilities

The end of the Cold War diminished the risk of nuclear conflagration, but it also brought an upsurge of conflicts of other kinds. These have created new roles and challenges for armed forces, intelligence agencies, police forces and other government agencies. The Gulf War of 1991 was followed by a series of conflicts in the Balkans, the growth of international terrorism and the wars in Afghanistan and Iraq – and these are just some of the conflicts detailed each year in the *Chart of Conflict*, published with *The Military Balance*, the annual IISS assessment of states' military capabilities. The nature of the conflicts, the capabilities that are required to bring them to a peaceful conclusion and the strategic challenges that they pose are constant themes in the work of the IISS. Since the 2001 attacks on the United States, which brought the threat of international terrorism into sharp focus, the conflicts in Afghanistan and Iraq have demanded particular attention.

A striking characteristic of 2008 was that events in Iraq received far less international attention than they had in the five years following the American-led invasion of 2003. This was despite the fact that, although a change in American military tactics had helped to reduce violence, Iraq remained a dangerous place. Meanwhile, the situation in Afghanistan was seen as a growing crisis that would require the devotion of additional foreign military and civilian resources. Casualties caused by the Taliban insurgency were mounting and the quality of governance by Afghan institutions remained alarmingly poor.

Francesc Vendrell, a Spanish diplomat with long experience of Afghanistan, brought a particularly candid assessment of the international community's performance in that country to the IISS Global Strategic Review in Geneva in September. Vendrell was the EU special representative for Afghanistan from 2002 to 2008, and had previously been the UN secretary-general's representative in Kabul. The situation, he told the conference, was 'worse than it has been since 2001'. He listed at least seven failures on the part of the international community that had, in his view, led to this. Among these were a 'light footprint' that had allowed the Taliban to regroup, and a 'blindness towards Pakistan'. Vendrell said:

> I think we should not have taken President Pervez Musharraf at his word when he promised a wholesale change in Pakistani policy towards Afghanistan. The result is that only now have we come round to realising that we cannot solve the Afghan problem without also resolving the issue of the support that has until recently been given to the Taliban by Pakistan's Inter-Services Intelligence [agency] or elements within it, and without now also sorting out the problem of extremism in Pakistan itself.

At NATO's April 2008 summit in Bucharest, leaders agreed on a vision for Afghanistan that included a 'comprehensive approach by the international community, bringing together civilian and military efforts'. They said that 'Euro-Atlantic and wider international security is closely tied to Afghanistan's future as a peaceful, democratic state' and that the NATO mission there was their 'top priority'. There is no doubt that the credibility of the NATO alliance, which has a 50,000-strong force in Afghanistan, is closely tied to the setting of clear goals for the country's future, and to their eventual attainment. Vendrell reiterated the need for a comprehensive policy, but said that it should encompass the entire region, including Pakistan, Iran and India. The military presence should, he believed, continue for as long as the Afghan public through its elective representatives wanted it to, but should be backed by a Status of Forces Agreement, as in Iraq.

Conflicts such as those in Afghanistan and Iraq have proved an extreme test of the military capabilities of the nations that have deployed troops to them. These experiences have prompted deep thought among military commanders about capabilities required in the modern age. This has also been an important theme of work at the IISS, which published in 2008 a Strategic Dossier on *European Military Capabilities: Building Armed Forces for Modern Operations*. The 2008 IISS Global Strategic Review was fortunate to have as speakers two serving officers who had held commands in Afghanistan: General David Richards, the British Army's commander-in-chief, Land Forces and, previously, commander of the NATO International Security Assistance Force (ISAF); and Lieutenant-General Karl Eikenberry of the US Army, deputy chairman of the NATO Military Committee and former commander of the US-led Coalition forces of *Operation Enduring Freedom*.

Richards said that militaries were facing their 'horse and tank moment' – the equivalent for contemporary military staffs of the challenges faced by officers in the 1920s who 'struggled … to understand that the era of the horse had been replaced by that of the tank'. Conflict in the Middle East had rapidly transformed the outlook of the British Army. Ten years ago, 'it was tanks and fast jets that dominated tactical doctrine'. Today, Richards said, the military lexicon was 'expeditionary logistics, unmanned aerial vehicles, precision attack, protection, helicopters, engineers, lasers, combat logistic patrols, chemical, biological, radiological and nuclear defence, electronic warfare, intelligence fusion, and understanding and influencing one's environment'.

Europe's armed forces have been slow to adapt to the modern need for flexible, mobile deployable forces to confront non-state actors – this was emphasised by both the IISS Strategic Dossier on European military capabilities and the 2008 Adelphi Paper *European Military Crisis Management: Connecting ambition and reality*, by Bastian Giegerich. One reason for this is that they believe that they need to retain capabilities for state-to-state warfare and the guarding of national security, as opposed to for expeditionary operations. However, Richards's point was that the new capabilities to which he referred were also those that would be needed for more traditional operations: 'there is a good case for believing that even state-on-state warfare would be similar to that which we will be conducting against non-state groupings'.

Richards also emphasised the paramount need for a comprehensive approach: 'it is only when Europe's political leaders agree on mechanisms to allow all the levers of state power to be operated cohesively in a crisis or conflict that Europe will enjoy the strategic influence its size and wealth merits'. Missions such as that in Afghanistan, where the conflict was being conducted 'amongst the people', required plenty of 'boots on the ground'. At the same time, 'if you are using a lot of firepower, you are almost certainly losing'. Richards believed in addition that a great deal more coordination was needed, as well as much clearer command-and-control and better communication within multinational forces – 'Virtually every nation's security regime and architectures is a significant hindrance to operational command'.

For a senior British military officer, Richards made an unusual aside when he acknowledged that in developing a comprehensive approach, the European Union was 'potentially hugely more powerful in the new environment than traditional collective security organisations'. This was because it could in theory bring together political, economic and military power in a way that NATO could not. Eikenberry agreed that the EU had an advantage in delivering a comprehensive approach, but asked 'How much progress has it made in developing a truly expeditionary, non-military capability?'. The American general gave a critique of European security and defence policy. But there was an important contrast between his remarks and the US suspicion of EU entry into the security and defence arena of a decade ago. Washington is now fully supportive. As Eikenberry noted, 'the US's door is wide open for NATO–EU collaboration in the security domain, it appears wide open for a united Europe to walk through'.

However, it was clear that in his view, Europe was far from being able to engage in this way. There were deficiencies in its strategy, goals and capabilities. In security and defence, he said, 'it is not clear that Europe has a meaningful and coherent strategy that goes beyond its borders. There is clearly an overwhelming preference within Europe for soft power.' European countries duplicated each other's capabilities, for example in the area of logistics. In Afghanistan, he said, 'we have many great European forces ... but all with unique logistics requirements, because the equipment is not compatible, not interoperable'. It was not simply a matter of the amount of money being spent on defence, but of how it was being spent. Europe had failed to meet capability objectives and 'force generation remain[ed] extraordinarily difficult'.

Most advanced states' armed forces, facing international demands for foreign deployments, have been trying to accomplish more with less, as the budgetary resources available to them decline. The financial crisis of 2008 seemed likely to exacerbate these difficulties, as many governments faced the prospect of lower tax receipts because of an economic slowdown, and higher spending in order to keep struggling economies going. Defence budgets appeared an obvious likely casualty of this squeeze, and this will perhaps further inhibit the ability of Western states to manage the world's problems and conflicts through military intervention. On the other hand, a budget squeeze could also force a higher level of cooperation between states' armed forces, since it could encourage them to reduce duplication in spending and obtain efficiencies through more coordinated capabilities.

Amid such calls for further transformation of capabilities in order to meet new threats, there was also a reminder in 2008 that more classic strategic confrontations, and enmities going back hundreds of years, should not be forgotten. Russia's heavy-handed response to mounting tensions with Georgia revived twentieth-century worries about national security in several European countries.

Classic confrontations and new balances

In August 2008, Russia poured troops and tanks into Georgia, proclaiming outrage at a Georgian attack on Tskhinvali, capital of South Ossetia, which had long claimed independence from Georgia. Georgia's military, which had been undergoing modernisation to NATO standards in preparation for joining the alliance – an ambition heavily sponsored by the Bush administration – saw its bases destroyed. The humiliating outcome for Tbilisi was that two separatist territories – Abkhazia, as well as South Ossetia – were definitively removed from its control and had their declarations of independence recognised by Moscow. Russian President Dmitry Medvedev and his predecessor Vladimir Putin, now prime minister, defiantly dared the world to do what it might in response.

John Chipman, the director-general and chief executive of the IISS, was clear that the Russia–Georgia conflict 'does not usher in a new Cold War'. Speaking at the launch of the IISS's *Strategic Survey 2008* in September, he said that the events of August should prompt new thinking in Western capitals about what approach to Russia would best serve their interests. Enlargement of NATO, he said, should take place if it was in the service of the Alliance's strategic interests, but not as a priority in itself. 'NATO must not transform its expansion policy into a game of Russian roulette', he said. The West needed a policy towards Russia that determined 'what interests are worth defending and in what manner, and on what issues it may still be possible to collaborate with Russia in order to induce more congenial behaviour in other areas'. Noting that even Russia's own allies had not joined it in recognising the breakaway territories, Chipman cautioned that 'a bit of old-fashioned sangfroid is called for in these unfortunately quite old-fashioned strategic times'.

Oksana Antonenko, IISS senior fellow for Russia and Eurasia, has been closely involved in the South Ossetian problem, having for two and a half years led a mediation process that brought Georgian and South Ossetian officials together in a dialogue. Addressing the IISS Global Strategic Review, she said that the August conflict had 'nothing at all to do with the Cold War' and that use of such language was very unhelpful to resolving the crisis. The core of the problem was the centuries-old Georgian–Ossetian conflict, and it was not at all surprising that this 'frozen' conflict had flared up again. While it had been Georgia's 'overwhelming and indiscriminate use of force against civilians in Tskhinvali' that had prompted Russia's military response, Moscow had gone too far in occupying and bombing parts of 'Georgia proper'. Among the issues that needed to be addressed now was the creation of new means for Russia and the West to address in a positive manner the key international issues that we face today, such as non-proliferation, conflict resolution and arms control. We are in a situation now in which both Russia and the West are engaged, not so much in a zero-sum game, but a negative-sum one.

John Chipman's call for a new assessment of what was in the West's strategic interests came two months before Americans elected Barack Obama, a man promising new approaches of all kinds, to be their next president. Obama will take over after a period of profound dysfunction in world affairs, in which George Bush's global response to the murder of 3,000 people on 11 September 2001 found few admirers in Europe. In Iraq, under the slogan of a 'global war on terror', the United States sought to launch a re-making of the Middle East through democratisation and the ending of tyrannies. This proved overambitious in both strategy and execution. The administration's final year, as Chipman said, 'saw grey returning as the main colour on the diplomatic palette, pushing the presumed certainties of black and white to the sidelines'. As he put it, 'the idealistic and entrepreneurial mode of Western foreign policy is over. How idealism and realpolitik will intermingle in the future will hugely depend on the personality of the future US president.'

In dealing with a host of challenges and conflicts, Obama will have the opportunity to open new avenues and to strike new balances and bargains, even as he pursues American national-security objectives that will remain, when all is said and done, extremely similar to what they have been for many years. But after Bush, America's strategic potency is much less taken for granted in the world. The United States remains, as Chipman said, 'the "swing" geopolitical player, the one that by its action or inaction can have the most impact on the comity of nations and the stability of the international system as a whole'. But international diplomatic activity will now be more plural. 'America is unable now to shape the international agenda alone, and needs international partners.' It is Obama's challenge to engage these partners – but it is their challenge to play their full part as well.

Perspectives on Asia

Outside Europe, the United States' most important current and potential political and security partners are to be found in Asia. This huge region will, however, also be a source of key challenges for Obama's administration. According to some observers, one significant consequence of the global economic crisis of 2008 will be that the economic and political power and influence of the East will increase relative to that of the West. But while it is true that many Asian economies have thrived during the current decade, in some cases making remarkable recoveries from the depredations of the 1997–98 Asian financial crisis, it also the case that Asia is far from constituting a bloc in any sense: its constituent states mainly remain highly sovereign in their outlook. Indeed, although intensifying trade, investment and the movement of workers and tourists are transforming Asia from its traditional essential status of a geographically defined construct of Western onlookers into a region built on common economic interests, it remains beset by inter-state tensions. These tensions – and the related potential for inter-state conflict – seem unlikely to dissipate, as major Asian powers continue to grow, not only economically, but also in terms of their political confidence and willingness to assert their power, which in some cases will include an important military component.

During 2008, there was a particularly strong Asian theme to the IISS's schedule of international meetings, at which delegates discussed in depth the key security issues of concern both to governments in the region and to external stakeholders. As well as the seventh in the series of IISS Shangri-La Dialogues in Singapore, the Institute also staged its first India Global Forum in New Delhi and organised conferences with local think tanks in Japan and the Republic of Korea. While these meetings' agendas were broad, the themes that stood out were the interlinked ones of challenges to the resilience of inter-state peace in Asia; the nature of major-power relations in the region, in particular the impact of the rise of China and India on the existing equilibrium; and the evolution of the regional architecture of institutions intended to enhance security collaboration. Presentations and discussion at these IISS meetings also highlighted the escalating importance of emerging security concerns – often summarised (not wholly accurately) as 'non-traditional' – such as those deriving from climate change.

Participants in IISS events during 2008 did not hear complete unanimity regarding the durability of the peace that has persisted between East Asian states for almost 30 years (and in South Asia since the 1999 Kargil war). Nevertheless, as a result of recent trends, there was certainly much optimism. Speaking at the Shangri-La Dialogue in late May, Singapore's prime minister, Lee Hsien Loong, remarked on positive developments in relations between North Korea and its interlocutors in the Six-Party Talks concerning its nuclear programme, between the 'key powers' in Asia (China, Japan and India), between China and Taiwan, and potentially between India and Pakistan. In his view, the Asian political landscape was 'generally benign'. US Secretary of Defense Robert Gates, also speaking at the Shangri-La Dialogue, concurred that 'overall trends' in Asia were 'positive', though he indicated a less upbeat view of 'North Korea's ambitions'. China's Lieutenant-General Ma Xiaotian, deputy chief of staff of the People's Liberation Army, declared that while diverse threats to peace – from territorial and maritime disputes, ethnic and religious tensions, 'expansion of military alliances', missile-defence developments, nuclear proliferation and 'space weaponisation' – persisted, the region's security was 'on the whole, in good shape', with relations between key powers 'constantly improving' and regional flashpoints becoming less dangerous. The key, according to Ma, was for powers in the region to recognise the importance of 'mutual respect and equality'.

In a presentation to the IISS–Japan Institute of International Affairs (JIIA) conference in Tokyo in June,[2] Australian academic and former senior public servant Hugh White painted a fundamentally less rosy picture of great-power relations in Asia. White challenged the optimism of many observers of East Asian security, arguing that because China's rise is simultaneous with the waning of US economic primacy, a new regional order is necessary to ensure that the presently 'incompatible political and strategic aims' of Washington and Beijing do not lead to major war. And White was not alone in his concern over the region's future security in terms of tensions and potential conflict between states. At the IISS Korea Forum in September, South Korean Prime Minister Han Seung-soo claimed that, while the prospects for inter-state war in Asia and elsewhere had 'never been as low as they are today', Asia was nevertheless the locus of strategic competition between major powers; at the same time, regional states were expanding their military power-projection capabilities, which increased the danger of new inter-state security dilemmas emerging. Like Han, US naval analyst and retired Rear Admiral Michael McDevitt, speaking at the IISS event in Tokyo, expressed concern over regional military trends. He was at pains to emphasise that 'offensive' military capabilities are often developed for reasons of deterrence and therefore do not necessarily indicate aggressive intent. Nevertheless, like White, McDevitt focused on the profound contradiction between US and Chinese strategy in East Asia. By enhancing its surveillance, submarine, maritime air and ballistic-missile capabilities, China was apparently attempting to deny US forces access to the East Asian littoral – access that the United States sees as vital in

---

[2]   Hugh White, 'Why War in Asia Remains Thinkable', *Survival*, December 2008–January 2009, pp. 85–104.

order to defend its interests and fulfil its obligations. In McDevitt's view, tension between China and the US over Taiwan would continue to fuel this 'capabilities competition' despite the détente between Beijing and Taipei that had been in evidence since the Kuomintang's Ma Ying-jeou became Taiwan's president in May. Ultimately, if China significantly circumscribed US military capacity, this would seriously undermine the credibility of Washington's regional security role.

Robert Gates used his headline Shangri-La Dialogue address above all to confront head-on those who thought that the wars in Iraq and Afghanistan had 'distracted' the US from its security role in Asia. The US defense secretary highlighted the United States' status as a Pacific nation and its concomitant 'enduring role' in Asia. More specifically, Gates enumerated the diverse ways in which the US played a part in enhancing regional states' security – notably as an ally, partner, 'resident power' and 'routine offshore presence'. Crucially – and perhaps presciently, given his own continuing role as secretary of defense in President Obama's cabinet – Gates also argued that the next US administration seemed 'certain' to continue existing security partnerships in Asia.

Just as the notion of American strategic decline in Asia and else-where has proved controversial, so there has also been debate over the prospective rise of China and India as major powers with global, as well as regional, influence. In general, few have disputed the notion that China's power, confidence and influence seem set to expand over the coming years and decades to affect not only Asia, but also the rest of the world. At the Shangri-La Dialogue, Singapore's Lee Hsien Loong pointed to China's 'increasingly crucial role' in regional and global affairs, and argued that it was already 'the most important player in Asia'. In his view, the Olympic Games in Beijing in August would be important as a gauge of China's confidence and competence in dealing with the world – and, in the event, the People's Republic carried off the event with panache, despite the earlier bad publicity resulting from disruptions to the Olympic torch relay around the world caused by clashes between pro-Beijing and pro-Tibet activists. Nevertheless, while the Shangri-La Dialogue address by Lieutenant-General Ma Xiaotian attested to growing confidence and will-ingness to engage more openly in debate over security matters, his stress on his country's domestic, regional and international threat perceptions provided a useful indication of Beijing's own perceived vulnerabilities and the fragility of China's status as a nascent superpower. The global economic crisis poses a new and serious challenge to China's rise: by late 2008, large sums of Chinese money had been lost in Western investment markets, declining demand from the West was causing Chinese factories to close, and the future of the rapid economic growth necessary to create employment and prosperity seemed in doubt.

India's rise as a major power seemed less than inevitable even before the effects of the economic crisis were felt. Smaller Asian states tend to see India as a benign power, whose role in regional affairs should be encouraged. Lee Hsien Loong, for example, spoke of India's growing weight in regional affairs, highlighting its extended naval reach, its negotiation of free-trade agreements in Southeast Asia and its expanding 'soft power'. Indian political leaders and commentators have tended to be rather more reserved when assessing their country's progress. Speaking at the 1st IISS–Citi India Global Forum in New Delhi in April, Foreign Secretary Shiv Shankar Menon pointed out that, despite 25 years of growth averaging 6% and India's far-reaching engagement in the global economy, 'daunting tasks' still faced India's government and society. Most important among these were the need to overcome mass poverty and to spread the benefits of growth throughout Indian society, particularly to the agricultural sector upon which the majority of Indians still depended. Infrastructural development was also necessary. Speaking at the same Forum, the Indian Prime Minister's Official Spokesman, Sanjaya Baru, agreed that 'for India to be a rising power, it must first resolve its economic challenges at home'. While Baru emphasised India's remarkable record of sustained economic growth and argued forcefully that this could be maintained despite the challenges still to be overcome (to which the impact of the global economic crisis and the urgent need for a more concerted approach to counter-terrorism in the wake of the attacks in Mumbai in late November 2008 must now be added), he left the question of 'whether we are a rising great power' for others to decide.

How successfully and peacefully regional states and other powers with vital interests and roles in the region cope with Asia's evolving power dynamics will depend in large part on the extent to which they can create viable regional institutions capable of mediating the inter-state tensions that will inevitably arise as waxing and waning powers attempt to assert and defend their interests. Events in recent years – such as the inadequacy of the Association of Southeast Asian Nations (ASEAN) in the face of the political crisis in Myanmar in late 2007 and the Thai–Cambodian border dispute a year later – have highlighted the weakness of the existing 'regional security architecture'. At the same time, there have been diverse efforts to institutionalise and intensify regional security cooperation through relatively new structures such as the ASEAN Defence Ministers' Meeting, the

East Asia Summit and the Shanghai Cooperation Organisation. Against this background, the question of how the regional security architecture might be made more effective arose repeatedly during the 2008 Shangri-La Dialogue and in the other Asian events organised by the IISS during the year.

Singapore has long been a driving force behind the intensification of regional cooperation in all forms, particularly through ASEAN. At the Shangri-La Dialogue, Prime Minister Lee Hsien Loong emphasised the role of ASEAN+3 (which involves China, Japan and South Korea as well as the ten members of ASEAN) and the East Asia Summit (which includes India, Australia and New Zealand as well as the members of ASEAN+3). Also speaking from a Singapore perspective, Minister of Defence Teo Chee Hean identified an evolving three-level regional security architecture.[3] This involved, at the top level, large, multilateral, pan-regional security forums such as the Shangri-La Dialogue and the ASEAN Regional Forum, bringing together all relevant contributors to regional security; at a middle level, sub-regional groupings such as ASEAN, the East Asia Summit, the South Asian Association for Regional Cooperation and the Shanghai Cooperation Organisation; and, finally, a third tier was made up of functional groups with more focused memberships for addressing specific challenges. Teo also emphasised the 'web of bilateral ties' that existed between Asia-Pacific countries, notably the United States' treaties and security partnerships, and the defence ties between certain combinations of ASEAN members. He argued that these layers of security cooperation all constituted important components of the regional security architecture.

Given the central role that the United States still plays in Asia-Pacific security, there was widespread acceptance at the Shangri-La Dialogue and other IISS meetings of the notion that the regional security architecture must involve all major actors in the region, whether their capital cities were located within or outside Asia. Taking the idea of inclusivity several steps further, Australian Prime Minister Kevin Rudd boldly entered the fray in 2008 with a proposal for an overarching Asia-Pacific Community. Rudd's idea appears to be akin to the notion of an Asian Concert of Power advanced by Hugh White at the IISS Tokyo conference. White viewed a 'concert' of power as an alternative to what he believed to be an emerging

---

3   Teo's speech is available at http://www.iiss.org/conferences/the-shangri-la-dialogue/ shangri-la-dialogue-2008/plenary-session-speeches-2008/sixth-plenary-session-modes-of-security-cooperation/sixth-plenary-session-teo-chee-hean/.

and potentially unstable regional *balance* of power, which could involve what Han Seung-soo called 'incessant struggles for dominance' – a balance would not rule out the possibility of major war as a balancing mechanism. However, both China and the United States would probably find it difficult to undertake the cooperation and concessions necessary for a 'concert' to work.

Discussion of Asia's security institutions will doubtless continue in the coming months and years, and may intensify. The IISS will seek to maintain its place close to the centre of this debate in the future.

Emerging security concerns

One theme that stood out from major IISS meetings during 2008 was the broadening agenda for defence and security policymakers. The Shangri-La Dialogue took place against the background of humanitarian emergencies following the impact of Cyclone Nargis on Myanmar and the Sichuan earthquake in China, in addition to rapid increases in fuel and food prices which had affected political stability in some Asia-Pacific states, and mounting global concern over the implications of climate change. A sense of the new importance to defence and security establishments of so-called 'non-traditional' concerns permeated the Dialogue's overall proceedings. In his keynote address, Lee Hsien Loong focused on the importance of 'common security challenges', notably the trend towards tighter supplies and higher prices of food, and the issue of humanitarian and disaster relief. Subsequent speakers took up these issues. Teo Chee Hean spoke of '360-degree' security challenges including energy, food and water security, humanitarian assistance and disaster relief and pandemics, as well as longer-established concerns over weapons proliferation, terrorism and maritime security. Indian Minister of State for Defence Pallam Raju reflected on the way that potential competition for energy, water and food injected substantial uncertainty into the future of global security. Indonesia's Widhwayan Prawiraatmadja highlighted Asia's rapidly growing demand for oil and the fact that even his country, a major oil producer, had become a net importer. As in many Asian countries, reducing fuel subsidies was necessary for economic reasons, but was affecting stability.

This emphasis on common security challenges inevitably stimulated considerable discussion of the necessity for common responses, particularly in relation to humanitarian and disaster relief. Such emerging security concerns provide 'motherhood and apple pie' rationales for cooperation between states that may be at loggerheads in other spheres of security. For most of the current decade, counter-terrorism has constituted such an issue. The results of counter-terrorism cooperation have been patchy, but there have been some success stories, for example in Indonesia, where support from Australian and US intelligence and law-enforcement agencies has severely curtailed local terrorist activity. Having emphasised the growing salience for defence planners of non-traditional threats, South Korean Minister of National Defence Lee Sang-hee called at the Shangri-La Dialogue for 'a crisis-management system of global reach' for coordinating the international response to natural disasters. Taking a regional perspective on the matter, Malaysian Deputy Prime Minister Dato' Sri Najib Tun Razak revisited his proposal, made at the 2006 Shangri-La Dialogue, for establishing a regionally based humanitarian-relief coordination centre, pointing to recent moves to set up an interim ASEAN Coordinating Centre for Humanitarian Assistance on Disaster Management to facilitate cooperation among regional states and international organisations. Najib argued that the disaster in Myanmar had been a test case for ASEAN's role in providing humanitarian assistance, and drew attention to the encouraging establishment of an ASEAN-led coordinating mechanism for the provision of international assistance to that country.

A question particularly pertinent to the concerns of Dialogue delegates was the proper role of armed forces in humanitarian assistance and disaster relief. Both Malaysia's Najib and Singapore's Teo Chee Hean argued that armed forces had important roles to play in this context. Jakob Kellenberger, president of the International Committee of the Red Cross, the inter-state organisation entrusted, primarily through the Geneva Conventions, with protecting the lives and dignity of victims of armed conflict, agreed that military personnel and logistic capabilities may play 'irreplaceable' disaster-relief roles, but also pointed out that the situation could be more complicated where humanitarian emergencies occurred in areas of conflict or in sensitive political contexts.

Humanitarian challenges in Asia and elsewhere are likely to grow as a result of changes in the physical environment. As Jeffrey Mazo of the IISS points out in his background paper on 'Asian Environmental Concerns' written for the IISS conference in Japan, climate change is likely to have a profound impact on Asia over the coming decades, particularly in terms of the effect of sea-level rise on human habitation of low-lying areas and declining food production. South Korean Prime Minister Han Seung-soo was undoubtedly right when he said that regarding environmental problems, Asia and the world now stood 'on the threshold of challenges that defy easy solutions'. As other IISS publications have explained, these environmental problems could generate highly significant and potentially destabilising security problems, in Asia and globally.[4] Investigating the security impact of environmental change will form an important part of the research agenda of the IISS as it moves into its second half-century.

Another area where the IISS has become increasingly actively involved in research and in encouraging debate is conflict resolution, which formed the main theme of its 2008 Global Strategic Review in Geneva. An area of particular interest for the Institute is the economic dimension of conflict resolution, which chairman of peace-promotion foundation the Portland Trust Ronald Cohen addressed with particular respect to the Middle East. Emphasising that 'economics are a necessary condition of conflict resolution', Cohen highlighted the work of the UK-based foundation in Israel and the Palestinian territories. While the enabling role of foreign governments and international organisations as donors would be key, Cohen particularly stressed the central part that private-sector investment could play in developing the Palestinian economy, which would also eventually benefit Israel in economic terms.

Of course, as Cohen pointed out, Palestine's extraordinarily high 'risk profile' continues to deter private-sector investment, and this is true of many conflict-prone regions. Indeed, as the spectrum of security threats worldwide has broadened over the present decade, there has been escalating interest from the business community as well as government in the assessment of political and security risks. However, as Nigel Inkster of the IISS pointed out in his dinner address to the IISS meeting in Korea, qualitative approaches may be a more effective means of assessing risk and planning responses to possible eventualities than the quantitative models that are currently enjoying voguish enthusiasm. Inkster, a former high-ranking British intelligence officer, is particularly well qualified to express extreme scepticism towards those who claim to be able to develop 'systems which will predict the future'. His view, doubtless shared by most IISS members, is that it is impossible to predict the future: 'there are too many variables and too many possible combinations, in addition to the uncertainties that arise from the vagaries of human behaviour'. Nevertheless, he cited Canadian academic Philip Tetlock's finding that 'cautious, pragmatic people whose instinct is to weigh the evidence carefully and not leap to premature conclusions' are rather better than most at assessing risk. Inkster argued that an open-minded approach to risk assessment should be embedded in corporate cultures.

---

[4]   See for example 'Climate Change: Security Implications and Regional Impacts', *Strategic Survey 2007* (Abingdon: Routledge for the IISS, 2007).

The most important implication of Inkster's presentation was that unexpected and inherently unpredictable events with strategic consequences will continue to occur. In his 2008 Alastair Buchan Memorial Lecture to the Institute, Michael Howard spoke of the world moving into what he called a 'post-Westphalian' epoch, in which the primary role of the state is increasingly to enable its people to participate in a transnational global order, rather than just to create and preserve an acceptable domestic order and defend it from rival states. It is as yet unclear what will be the effect on globalisation of the most severe global economic crisis for more than 70 years. But what is clear is that the world faces immense new challenges from environmental degradation and pressure on resources, and from non-state actors who often use violence in support of their causes. These factors may accentuate the unpredictability of international security affairs.

As addresses at major IISS events during 2008 have repeatedly suggested, in these circumstances, diverse kinds of new or revitalised international institutions will be key to meeting strategic challenges as varied as limiting climate change, countering terrorism, providing effective responses to humanitarian catastrophes, managing changing power dynamics in Asia, and preventing further nuclear proliferation. How this unpredictable and dangerous new world order might best be managed will be debated widely and intensely in the coming years, and the IISS – through its meetings around the world and its publications – will aim to play an important part in this debate.

I: Global Security Dynamics

Address to the IISS 50th Anniversary Dinner, London, 3 April 2008

Carl Bildt

Minister for Foreign Affairs, Sweden

Half a century ago, in 1958, we lived in a very different world indeed. The great wars of the first half of the century were still in living memory for most. There was something around called the Soviet Union. The year before it had stunned the world by launching a small beeping device called Sputnik that circled the globe. This was 'shock and awe' in an early incarnation. The year after, the 21st Congress of the Communist Party of the Soviet Union would trumpet the achievements of socialism and the imminent demise of capitalism. And there were many who believed – or feared – that this was the way the world was really going. We now know that at the time the United States still had more than ten times as many nuclear warheads as the Soviet Union. And we now know that it would be a few more years before the Soviet Union could get a couple of rudimentary ICBMs to stand up straight. But these years were the true beginning years of that race of fear that turned into the nuclear arms race which transformed the way we dealt with strategic affairs.

To say that much has changed during this half-century is certainly not an exaggeration. Back in the late fifties, my own country was actively planning to acquire nuclear weapons. In 1958, the supreme commander of the Swedish military was working on a plan to produce an arsenal of 100 nuclear warheads, beginning within six months of a planned 1965 start date for the programme, using two plutonium-producing reactors. Little thought – certainly none in public or political circles – was given to how these weapons would really be used, but the plan appears to have been for them to be used pre-emptively against a possible Soviet invasion fleet in the harbours of cities on the eastern and northern shores of the Baltic Sea. I can assure you that Sweden abandoned these plans, although it was a process that proceeded in stages and took some time. Gradually, 'thinking about the unthinkable', to use Herman Kahn's memorable words, produced a rational outcome. Thinking about the unthinkable also gradually changed the mentality in Washington and Moscow, and the twisted logic of the nuclear arms race gave way step-by-step to the complex politics of nuclear arms control and reductions. From a high point of more than 70,000 nuclear weapons in state arsenals around 1986, numbers have now been reduced to something in the order of 27,000.

The world is now indeed profoundly different from that of 1958. The cities that might then have been targets of planned Swedish nuclear weapons are today the cities and capitals of countries that are members of our European Union as well as of the North Atlantic Treaty Organisation (NATO). The peaceful demise of the Soviet Union is one of the truly defining features of our time. The disappearance of great empires is hardly unique – in the longer sweep of history, it is somewhat routine. But it is usually associated with strife, conflicts and major wars. In the wake of the uniquely peaceful implosion of the Soviet empire – though the decade of wars of disintegration in the Balkans must not be forgotten – we are now engaged in a truly historic attempt to build a genuinely new order of peace and prosperity in our part of the world – a Europe whole and free, democratic and dynamic, united by the rule of law anchored in our common institutions.

The importance of this can hardly be exaggerated. In the past century, it was the conflicts of Europe that twice spread over the globe and gave us worldwide wars. In the past century, it was the totalitarian ideas of Europe that spread over the world and produced carnage and suffering for millions. And in decades not long ago, it was the conflicts over this continent that risked producing that ultimate conflagration that prompted Albert Einstein to say that, while he was not certain which weapons the Third World War would be fought with, he knew that the Fourth World War would have to be fought with clubs and sticks. The building of this new order of peace and prosperity in our part of the world is still work in progress. Those of us attending the councils of the European Union or – as I did earlier today as an observer – the deliberations of the NATO Council can certainly testify to this. But if a Europe that in the past century produced models of wars for the world can instead produce a model for peace, I for one am of the opinion that it is worth all of these meetings – and much more.

That the collapse of the old order produced a new opportunity in a previously conflict-ridden Europe is undoubtedly a positive development. But as we widen our horizons, we are all aware of the major strategic challenges confronting us. There is no shortage of these. Tomorrow I am travelling to Tbilisi in the Caucasus to discuss situations that could easily produce very serious confrontations, possibly involving a resurgent Russia. In the days after, I will be in Hebron, Ramallah and Nablus on the West Bank of the Jordan River that has been under Israeli occupation for more than 40 years. The rivers of rage that run today through much of the vast Muslim world, from Morocco to Indonesia, fuelling the threat of global terrorism, have one of their major sources in our inability to resolve this painful conflict.

But if I had to identify the two most difficult strategic challenges that the international community will have to handle in the years ahead – apart from the obvious one of global terrorism – I would cite global climate change and nuclear proliferation. Both will require urgent attention in the next few years. I believe also that handling them will call for far-reaching changes to the structures of international cooperation.

During most of the decades of the IISS's existence, the nuclear calculations that needed to be made were those associated with the bipolarity between the US and the Soviet Union. The slow development of Chinese nuclear weapons did not fundamentally alter that situation, nor did the British or French arsenals, or what might be there in the sands of Israel. When both India and Pakistan demonstrated a nuclear capability in 1998, it meant a new and deeply disturbing development. The IISS has documented how Pakistan then became a source for the spread of sensitive nuclear technologies in the most dangerous directions. What we are faced with now is the danger of serious nuclear proliferation into more conflict-ridden and complex regions. It is not only a question of whether or not Iran gets the Bomb. A single state actor can still in all probability be handled with the logic of deterrence. But what lies ahead is the risk of a new phase in proliferation that will start with Iran and soon extend to one country and regime after another in the most conflict-ridden and volatile part of the world. Then, I fear that it will be only a matter of time before these weapons are used, either by a regime, in an act of desperation or miscalculation, or by one of the numerous non-state groups in the region. Most of us may still end our days without having seen a truly nuclear war. But the probability that our children will experience the use of these horrible weapons on a larger scale than in 1945 will be very high indeed. Clearly, this is something that we must give the highest-possible priority to preventing.

Thus the challenge is wider than just that of Iran and its quest for nuclear power, nuclear technology and possible nuclear weapons. Like Iran, one country after another is starting to talk about building nuclear power plants. Some – such as Egypt – are doing so because they have few alternatives for meeting the energy demands of rising populations and economic growth. Some – such as the Gulf states – are doing so because they see a need to preserve their petroleum resources for export and other uses in the future. Some are doing so as part of what they view as a necessary strategy for reducing fossil-fuel dependence and starting to tackle the challenges of climate change. Nuclear power remains controversial in many countries. This includes my own, although the issue is less flammable than it was some decades ago. Nevertheless, there is little doubt that we will see a considerable expansion of nuclear power in the decades ahead, and that it will be seen as one of the necessary responses to the climate-change challenge.

The link between civilian and military use of nuclear technology should not be exaggerated. Indeed, it was when civilian requirements for cheap and reliable electricity came to dominate Swedish nuclear programmes in the late 1950s and early 1960s that the military option became much more complicated and expensive. But the risks are there in the nuclear fuel cycle, particularly in the enrichment of uranium and the reprocessing of spent fuel that also produces plutonium. As there will be a larger number of nuclear reactors for power production in the decades ahead, including in volatile regions such as the Middle East, we must seek new ways to prevent the further spread of enrichment and reprocessing technologies. It is in these, not in nuclear technology or power as such, that the proliferation risks lie.

Thus, a critically important political challenge in the next few years must be to develop multinational and internationally controlled facilities for handling sensitive parts of the nuclear fuel cycle. Such a mechanism should seek to bring any new operations for uranium enrichment and plutonium separation under multinational control. Over time, these multinational controls would also extend to facilities that already existed, so as to ensure that all countries were treated equally in terms of their nuclear capabilities and to uncouple these fuel-cycle activities from their possible use as a strategic deterrent. Whether a concerted international approach to developing such mechanisms and institutions could also provide a framework within which a solution to the Iranian issue could be sought is a separate matter. If recent US intelligence estimates are to be believed – perhaps a daring assumption in these times – there would at least be some time to ponder this possibility and to explore its feasibility.

Although those who argue that there is no direct connection between the size of the nuclear arsenals of the US and Russia and the risk of proliferation are essentially correct, there is little doubt that further attempts to reduce existing arsenals would facilitate wider efforts to prevent further proliferation of nuclear weapons. Ample arguments for such a reduction also come from careful assessment of the usefulness of nuclear weapons in the modern world. The recent calls by George Shultz, Henry Kissinger, William Perry, Sam Nunn and others for a new policy on nuclear weapons are not the moralistic calls of the Campaign for Nuclear Disarmament of bygone days, but the rational conclusions of some of the best minds ever to have devoted their efforts to the subjects of national and international security. Their argument is based not only on the enormous risk that further proliferation of nuclear weapons represents, but also on the realisation that the military usefulness of these weapons is becoming more and more limited. Nuclear weapons are good for little more than very basic deterrence, and it is clear that the tasks of this nature that remain can be handled by arsenals far smaller than those of today. The emerging debate on these issues provides an important opportunity for moving ahead towards a new international consensus on radical cuts in nuclear arsenals – leading eventually to their elimination, a goal to which the nuclear powers have already committed themselves.

In the ongoing debates prior to the presidential elections in the US, all the remaining contenders have declared themselves in favour of seeking Senate ratification of the Comprehensive Nuclear Test-Ban Treaty. Early moves by a new administration in this direction would send a powerful signal of a new and promising line on these issues, and would pave the way for its ratification by other key nations. This should be coupled next year with new initiatives on the possibility of multinational nuclear fuel-cycle models. Perhaps this is an issue on which the European Union could take a lead in the global debate, in the same way as it has taken a lead in the debate on global cuts in carbon emissions.

On both the nuclear and climate issues, there will be a need to reform key international institutions. In both cases, a more effective multilateralism is clearly called for. A multinational nuclear-fuel regime might call for a new role for the International Atomic Energy Agency or for the setting up of an entirely new international mechanism. A truly effective global treaty to limit carbon emissions might well call for far-reaching new international mechanisms in the financial field, as well as elsewhere. We might need a new International Nuclear Fuel Authority as well as a new International Climate and Environmental Financing Authority – or an evolution of existing institutions in these directions.

To move in these directions, in order to help to handle two of the most pressing global challenges of today, will require strong global political leadership. The world is different today from how it was only a few years ago. The role of the United States remains indispensable. The role of the European Union is clearly growing in importance. We have an interest in keeping Russia engaged in constructive global diplomacy. Japan remains a key member of the G8. But on issues like these, it is clear that we cannot move forward without actively engaging countries like China, India and Brazil. As we move forward with the new solutions demanded by the new challenges, we may well find we also need new institutions for global governance, beyond the G8 and in parallel with those offered by the United Nations.

Address to the IISS, London, 23 July 2008

Preventing a New Age of Nuclear Insecurity

William Hague

Shadow Foreign Secretary, United Kingdom

Two years ago, I gave a speech here at the IISS in which I warned of a crisis in the global non-proliferation regime caused by the actions of countries like Iran and North Korea, the nuclear black market, the threat of nuclear terrorism and stalemate over the future of the Nuclear Non-Proliferation Treaty (NPT). I called on the international community to overcome its divided and uncertain response to these challenges. Since then, while there have been some welcome developments, the crisis over nuclear proliferation has grown.

Nowhere is this more evident than in the Middle East. International sanctions and diplomacy have failed so far to stop Iran's nuclear programme. The United States government has presented evidence that Syria was constructing a secret nuclear reactor with North Korean technology and assistance. And two weeks ago, Iran test-fired a range of missiles aimed at demonstrating that it can disrupt oil flows through the Strait of Hormuz and target Israel, US forces in Iraq and even parts of Europe. Israel has also conducted long-range military exercises that were widely portrayed as a dry run for a bombing mission against Iran's nuclear installations.

Given these events, some might argue that this is the wrong time to talk about the NPT, and that governments should concentrate all their efforts on the crisis over Iran. However, I believe that it is precisely this tendency to deal with each proliferation crisis as a one-off that fundamentally hampers our ability to stem the global spread of nuclear weapons. In the space of relatively few years we have been confronted by confirmed nuclear-weapons programmes in Iraq, North Korea and Libya, and concealed nuclear activities and a suspected nuclear-weapons programme in Iran. While all these cases are different, they have important features in common – including how these countries acquired their technology, how they hid their activities (in the case of Iran, for nearly two decades), and how they successfully held off international pressure for many years.

With every prospect of the pace of nuclear proliferation increasing, we must lift our gaze to look at the coming crises, not just the current one. The certainties of the Cold War, when nuclear weapons were concentrated in the hands of a few and mutually assured destruction prevailed, have been replaced by a far more unpredictable array of threats. We are facing a new era of nuclear insecurity that, left unchecked, could lead to the unravelling of the NPT, which has been a fundamental pillar of our global security for the last four decades. We therefore must act now while time is still on our side and while there is a remaining chance of turning this tide.

Since I last spoke on this subject, there has been a resurgence of interest in nuclear-weapons issues. On the other side of the Atlantic, George Shultz, Henry Kissinger, William Perry and Sam Nunn have proposed an initiative to 'reverse reliance on nuclear weapons globally … and ultimately end them as a threat to the world', which has drawn attention from around the globe. It has given much-needed intellectual force and impetus to the debate about how to make the world safer from nuclear weapons and has attracted the support of leading figures from the worlds of defence, politics and academia, including in this country.

The two US presidential candidates have also both given major speeches on the need to make nuclear non-proliferation a higher priority. Senator John McCain has committed himself to reducing the size of the US nuclear arsenal 'to the lowest number' needed to maintain US security and commitments. Senator Barack Obama has spoken of the need for 'deep cuts' in US and Russian nuclear stockpiles. Both have embraced the vision of a world free of nuclear weapons.

We welcome the fact that these ideas are being debated in the United States, the country with the largest number of operationally active nuclear warheads in the world and stockpiles second only to Russia's, and a country whose weight and influence is indispensable to the success of any global initiative.

We also welcome the specific proposals put forward by Shultz, Kissinger, Perry and Nunn for changes to the Cold War posture of deployed nuclear weapons to reduce the danger of an accidental or unauthorised use, for action to secure global stocks of fissile material, and for substantial reductions in the size of nuclear forces in all states that possess them – something that the UK has already undertaken.

Addressing the existence of stockpiles of nuclear weapons is an integral part of efforts to reduce the risks of nuclear weapons and a fundamental commitment under the NPT, which requires negotiations 'in good faith on effective measures' on nuclear disarmament and on 'a treaty on general and complete disarmament under strict and effective international control'. Britain has an excellent record. We have reduced our nuclear capability to a single system and the explosive power of our nuclear arsenal by 75% since the Cold War, more than any other nuclear-weapons power, and the government has recently proposed using Britain as a 'laboratory' to explore how disarmament could be verified. Showing that we take our disarmament commitments seriously is a vital part of winning the moral argument against nuclear proliferation.

However, no amount of nuclear disarmament will protect us from the dangers of nuclear weapons without a more comprehensive approach to nuclear proliferation, which is by far the biggest challenge we face today. There is an urgent need for a concerted effort to put the brakes on nuclear proliferation, without which steps towards reducing nuclear stockpiles worldwide will have little effect.

The evidence for this is clear: more countries have acquired or attempted to acquire nuclear-weapons technology despite progress that has already been made in reducing nuclear stockpiles worldwide. The US and Russia, which together possess 95% of the world's nuclear weapons, have destroyed over 13,000 warheads between them since 1987. It is a little-known and startling fact that one in ten homes, schools and businesses in the US receives electricity generated from dismantled Russian nuclear warheads and by 2013, the equivalent of 20,000 warheads will have been turned into nuclear fuel – enough to power the entire United States for about two years. Concrete and progressive steps to reduce arsenals have been taken, without denting the trend towards an increasing number of nuclear-weapons states.

Although some countries have renounced nuclear-weapons programmes or given up nuclear weapons on their soil, there are many more nuclear-weapons powers today than there were at the time of the creation of the NPT, which aimed to limit the possession of nuclear weapons to five recognised powers: the United States, Russia, China, Britain and France. Today the global picture is far more complex, with Israel an undeclared nuclear power that has not signed the NPT, Pakistan and India declared nuclear powers also outside the treaty, and North

Korea having pulled out of the treaty and declared itself a de facto nuclear power. In the light of this, not only is achieving nuclear disarmament now far harder than it was even at the height of the Cold War, but the risks of nuclear confrontation and the spread of nuclear technology are greater. Furthermore, unilateral disarmament by one or more of the nuclear-weapons states would not change the rationale that drives some countries to seek nuclear capability.

Take the example of Iran. The driving factors behind Iran's nuclear programme – the country's relative weakness in conventional forces, its perception of being militarily encircled and its desire to ensure the survival of the Revolution – will remain whether or not the US and Russia make further reductions in their respective stockpiles. Iran knows full well that it cannot match the US or Israel in conventional forces, and that its position would be significantly altered if it had its own deterrent. This bigger picture of an uncertain world is also why I believe that the UK is right to take steps to retain its minimum strategic nuclear deterrent and why the Conservative Party supports the decision to renew the *Trident* submarines. In short, proliferation, not the risk of accidental or deliberate nuclear war between the five original nuclear powers, is the greatest threat we face today.

There are five major sources of this new threat. First, the barriers to becoming a nuclear-weapons power are considerably lower now than they were in the past. It was previously the case that only the most advanced nations had the technological capability to develop a nuclear-weapons programme. This is no longer true. Although we have not yet reached the state predicted by President Eisenhower half a century ago – 'the knowledge possessed by several nations will eventually be shared by others, possibly all others' – it is increasingly likely to become a reality. Much of the most significant nuclear technology is 50 years old, and up to 40 countries are now considered to have the technical know-how to produce nuclear weapons.

Secondly, a thriving black market exists, operating as a one-stop shop for would-be nuclear powers, so that those countries, such as Libya, that did not have the indigenous base for a nuclear-weapons programme were able to import it from abroad, leapfrogging the years of complex research and development normally needed. Former CIA director George Tenet has argued that 'in the current marketplace, if you have a hundred million dollars, you can be your own nuclear power'. Four years after the discovery of the operations of the rogue Pakistani scientist A.Q. Khan – who Tenet described as 'at least as dangerous as Osama bin Laden' – we are still trying to piece together the extent of his network, which spanned 30 different countries. Only last month, encrypted documents on a computer seized from Swiss members of the network revealed a design for a compact nuclear device that could be fitted onto a ballistic missile; an advanced system that no one had known that A.Q. Khan was supplying. More ominously still, we do not know who may have bought these designs, or how many other copies exist. Only a fraction of the black market has been exposed and few people have been successfully prosecuted. We are also behind the curve in learning how to catch and expose these individuals, who are more likely to be engineers and businessmen than the terrorists of popular imagination.

Thirdly, it is no longer beyond the power of terrorist groups to acquire the nuclear material necessary to detonate a nuclear device in one of our cities. We face the nightmarish combination of insecure nuclear research reactors and stockpiles of nuclear material across the world, coupled with porous borders and international terrorist groups known to have sought nuclear capability. Russia is a particular focus of this concern, as its stockpiles are widely dispersed and in some cases believed to be poorly guarded. Pakistan is another source of worry. The director general of the International Atomic Energy Agency (IAEA) recently warned that 'there are no grounds for the international community to consider relaxing its vigilance' over the threat of nuclear terrorism, the consequences of which would obviously be devastating beyond anything we have yet encountered in the long catalogue of terrorist atrocities.

Fourthly, we have to grapple with the dangers of the nuclear fuel cycle. Once a country knows how to produce enriched uranium for a civilian power programme, it has overcome one of the greatest obstacles to acquiring a nuclear weapon. It can undertake such enrichment while remaining a member of the NPT, allowing it to 'cheat' the treaty, as North Korea did. Not only is it extremely difficult to detect the moment when a state possessing civilian nuclear power decides to switch to a secret nuclear-weapons programme, the international community is also then left with very little time to react. Countries no longer even need to continue all the way to a nuclear test, but can linger on the threshold, being 'virtual' nuclear-weapons powers with the ability to assemble a weapon at very short notice.

At which stage, therefore, should we be alarmed? There were jitters when 13 countries in the Middle East announced new or revived plans to pursue or explore civilian nuclear energy in the space of 11 months between 2006 and 2007. Most will probably choose to buy their nuclear fuel on the international market, but some may wish to develop the full fuel cycle, as Iran is doing. If Iran does emerge as a nuclear power on their doorstep, would they then feel compelled to pursue their own nuclear-weapons programmes? The combination of high oil prices, finite oil reserves and climate change means that increasing numbers of countries will consider nuclear power to meet their energy needs. The dilemma of the fuel cycle is one that will only get worse. As things stand, we do not have an answer.

Finally, the absence of effective control of proliferation has contributed to the reluctance of nuclear-weapons powers to assist with the transfer of peaceful nuclear technology to states that want it. This reluctance has undermined the central bargain of the NPT, that states which promised not to pursue nuclear weapons would receive access to nuclear energy for peaceful purposes as an 'inalienable right'. As a result, non-nuclear-weapons states feel they have lost out on the promised advantages of the NPT, and the international consensus about how to address nuclear threats has been weakened.

Every five years, all members of the NPT meet to review the progress of the treaty. The last review conference, in 2005, was so mired in disagreement that it could not even agree a final document. In the words of former UN Secretary-General Kofi Annan, '"mutually assured destruction" has been replaced by mutually assured paralysis. This sends a terrible signal of disunity and waning respect for the treaty's authority. It creates a vacuum that can be exploited.' Iran has played on perceptions that non-nuclear-weapons states have been denied access to technology by presenting itself as a champion of the rights of developing states and pledging to share its nuclear technology with others, implying that this is a dispute about access to technology rather than about Iran's violation of the NPT.

It is this serious proliferation crisis which the international community has not so far addressed with sufficient rigour, and which requires a new concerted approach. This is not a problem that has arisen overnight to take the world by surprise. The warning has been written loud and clear in the actions of Iran and North Korea, in the blunt responses of countries that say privately that if Iran goes nuclear, they will have no choice but to consider their options, and in the bulletins of intelligence communities that tell us that terrorists continue to try to acquire the means to inflict mass casualties.

The international community has given the impression of fire-fighting in the wake of each crisis, with no consistent approach. North Korea has been dealt with through the Six-Party Talks, largely outside the UN Security Council. Iran was dealt with initially by the European 'troika' of

Britain, France and Germany; it then moved to the Security Council, and is now handled by the so-called 'P5+1', the five permanent members of the Security Council plus Germany. But proliferation problems cannot forever be solved one country at a time. What would happen if we were suddenly faced by five or six cases of proliferation simultaneously, as could conceivably happen if Iran successfully acquired a nuclear weapon? How would we prevent the risk of nuclear war when 'new' nuclear-weapons powers, unconstrained by experience, civil–military checks and balances or arms-control agreements, came into conflict? We only have to think about what the world could look like in five years to understand why we have to do better: these problems will become more difficult to respond to, in a more challenging global environment and with increasing calls on our diplomats, soldiers and resources.

In short, we cannot deal only with the known threats posed by existing nuclear stockpiles; we must also address the reality of the proliferation threat as it evolves and becomes less predictable and even more dangerous. I want at this point to set out eight proposals which I believe the British government should adopt and champion publicly now.

First, there needs to be strategic dialogue between Britain, the United States, France, Russia and China on how to achieve future reductions in nuclear stockpiles, on ways to reduce further the risk of nuclear confrontation or accidental nuclear war, and on how to make progress on our disarmament commitments in a way that strengthens the NPT. Britain should propose a conference of the five recognised nuclear-weapons powers that should take place before the 2010 NPT Review Conference to seek agreement.

Secondly, Britain should launch a new effort to address the decline of the NPT and restore the broken consensus at its heart, with the goal of making the 2010 NPT Review Conference a success after ten years of failure and recriminations. We cannot hope to build better understanding and cooperation between nuclear and non-nuclear states unless we engage with countries which have not pursued a nuclear weapon even though they are considered to have the capability to do so, such as Argentina, Brazil and Japan. These are some of the prominent non-nuclear-weapons states and our natural partners in addressing these issues. As part of the drive to reinvigorate the NPT, we should also aim to bring the three nuclear powers outside its remit – India, Pakistan and Israel – within the wider non-proliferation regime.

Thirdly, there are specific steps which must be taken to close the loopholes in the NPT. We must seek agreement about how to respond when a country either commits a serious breach of the NPT or withdraws from it altogether. At the moment, there is no automatic procedure whereby a breach of the treaty will be referred to the Security Council. This means that valuable time that could be spent addressing a suspected nuclear-weapons programme is lost in political dispute about whether the Security Council should be discussing the matter at all. It took two years after Iran's secret nuclear programme was exposed to the world for the issue to be referred to the Security Council, and many further months for UN sanctions to finally be agreed. Iran has continued its programme almost uninterrupted throughout this period, with the result that it has all but acquired the ability to enrich uranium to the level needed for a nuclear weapon. There needs to be a mechanism, preferably a Security Council resolution, that would automatically refer a country to the Security Council in the event of a serious breach of the NPT.

The international community is also powerless to respond when a country withdraws from the NPT, as North Korea did. While the sovereign right of any country to withdraw from a treaty has to be respected, the NPT is not like any other treaty, and the risks associated with its abuse are uniquely dangerous. This could be addressed by a UN resolution that would immediately trigger discussions at the Security Council if a country withdrew from the NPT or announced that it would do so. The IAEA would be required to report immediately on the nuclear activities of that country and on whether there were grounds to suspect that it was concealing a nuclear-weapons programme. The resolution could also include the provision for international sanctions if the country in question were found to have breached the NPT.

Fourthly, we have to agree a mechanism to bring the nuclear fuel cycle under international control. High oil prices and mounting concern about climate change will make nuclear energy more attractive to many, just as burgeoning populations and growing economies in the developing world will make it increasingly necessary to many. We are already seeing an increased demand for the construction of new nuclear facilities worldwide, as well as for the supply of enriched uranium to power them. Proliferation control needs to keep pace with this fast-changing reality. Whether control mechanisms take the form of international partnerships between a small number of states producing nuclear fuel, or a network of 'fuel banks', proposals must be adopted and implemented as soon as is practicable. Britain should make this one of the top priorities of its international diplomacy. Addressing the dangers of the nuclear fuel cycle will make it possible to launch wider efforts to make the peaceful applications of nuclear technology available to all those countries that desire them.

Fifthly, we need to strengthen the IAEA and the international system of safeguards and inspections. We need to face the fact that the existing inspections regime was unable to detect the covert programmes of Iraq, Libya or Iran. After over four years of inspections, we still do not know the extent of Iran's nuclear programme or any activities it may be concealing. We still cannot be sure that Iran does not have secret sites where it is enriching uranium or conducting weaponisation studies. This hampers our diplomacy and, indeed, increases the risk of military confrontation. At the 2010 Review Conference, the Additional Protocol, which gives the IAEA extra inspection powers, ought to be made a universal requirement for all countries within the NPT. The momentum for this needs to be developed now.

We must also ensure that the IAEA has the resources it needs. The IAEA monitors hundreds of tonnes of nuclear material in hundreds of facilities across the world, to ensure that material is not diverted from civilian to military purposes. It has sounded a warning about its ability to maintain this important work over the long term, since the amount of nuclear material that it has to monitor has increased more than tenfold since the 1980s, while its budget has remained virtually static. Indeed, as one report noted, the safeguards budget of the IAEA is not more than the budget of the police department of the city in which it is located. We have a vital interest in making sure that the Agency's budget will be able to sustain the growing demands it will face, and we have to ensure that member states are devoting sufficient resources to it.

Sixthly, we must urgently improve the international ability to track and block the trade in nuclear-weapons technology and isolate countries engaged in these practices. For an example of why this is important, one only has to look at Iran's missile capability, which includes *Shahab*-3 missiles based on North Korean technology that may one day give Iran the ability to threaten Europe. Part of the solution must lie in increasing our ability to interdict suspect vessels carrying such material. Interdiction currently happens on an informal basis under the Proliferation Security Initiative (PSI), which is a set of principles to which member states adhere and resolve to 'seriously consider' boarding suspect vessels of another state. The PSI does not impose mandatory steps on its members. It also has no international secretariat, no shared databases and no established funding. This flexibility might be a strength, but it does not guarantee its sustainability. The PSI's reach is also limited. Key countries such as

Malaysia, Indonesia and Pakistan remain outside the initiative, as do India, China and South Korea. The urgent need to counter proliferation from North Korea makes it vital that we increase Asian participation in the PSI, as well as that of other important countries that still do not participate. To do this, we must find ways of making the initiative more acceptable to those countries currently opposed to involvement.

The seventh proposal is that we must act to disrupt the financial networks that support the proliferation of weapons of mass destruction. Identifying and blocking these activities is essential as a means to slow down illicit nuclear programmes and to put pressure on the governments behind them. The Iranian regime, for example, has been accused of disguising its hand in terrorism and weapons proliferation by using front companies and intermediaries to obtain dual-use technology and materials. The UN Security Council decided in 2007 to ban a major Iranian bank, Bank Sepah, from the international financial system. The Financial Action Task Force has also warned that Iran's lack of money-laundering and counter-terrorism controls means that it poses a significant threat to the international financial system. These developments have had a significant effect on the willingness of international banks and companies to do business with Iran and have increased the isolation of the regime. We await the Financial Action Task Force's report on proliferation finance, which will study the techniques and trends of proliferation finance, and provide recommendations to all governments on how to address the threat. Building on these recommendations, we must urgently develop the capacity at a national and international level to isolate nuclear proliferators from the international financial system. We must ensure that we have the right expertise and experience within our government departments to keep on top of this fast-expanding area and the capacity to assist other countries that do not have the means to do so. Many countries have been unable to meet their obligations under UN resolutions to establish domestic laws and controls against the proliferation of weapons of mass destruction. This must be addressed, as our collective security against nuclear proliferation or a nuclear attack could be shattered by a single point of vulnerability.

Finally, we must deal more resolutely with existing cases of nuclear proliferation, learning the lessons of Libya and North Korea. First and foremost, this means a step change in the international community's response to Iran's nuclear programme. The components of a successful diplomatic strategy have been slowly and painfully assembled, in the form of limited sanctions and a diplomatic offer holding out the prospect of normalisation of relations and economic benefits if a long-term settlement is reached.

However, there has yet to be any breakthrough comparable to North Korea's recent symbolic destruction of the notorious Yongbyon tower at its main atomic reactor and its declaration of its nuclear facilities. Success in persuading Libya to relinquish its nuclear programme and recent progress with North Korea were the result of an intensity of diplomacy, incentives and isolation that we have yet to muster on Iran.

In the Conservative Party we have argued that the ability of the US to dangle carrots in front of Iran requires Europe to wield a bigger stick. In particular, Britain and other European nations should ban new investment in Iranian oil and gas, and the use of export credits to subsidise trade with Iran. As a part of the strategy for dealing with Iran, Britain should also increase its level of dialogue with Middle Eastern and particularly Gulf countries most affected by Iran's nuclear programme, to address their security concerns and gain their fullest possible support for international sanctions.

The need for further decreases in nuclear stockpiles and work towards a world free of the fear of the use of nuclear weapons is as important a goal as tackling global warming. But a strategy to achieve this goal must go beyond unilateral action by the nuclear-weapons states. Nuclear weapons are no longer a stand-alone issue in relations between the great powers, but are bound up with wider issues of energy security, regional security, regional power and action by non-state actors. Our strategy for dealing with nuclear proliferation needs to be commensurately broad.

The NPT is the world's most upheld treaty – only four states are not members. It has entrenched a consensus that nuclear weapons are among the most dangerous threats to our planet, and that reducing these dangers requires the efforts of all countries. We must not allow it to be fatally undermined by threats that its makers could not have predicted. Governments, including our own, have to accord counter-proliferation the highest priority. Reducing the risk posed by weapons of mass destruction and nuclear weapons in particular is not a party-political issue, but a vital national interest which needs a common purpose and shared vision. We welcome the steps that the British government has taken to put Britain at the forefront of the debate on nuclear reductions and to propose a means of bringing the fuel cycle under international control. But such action now needs to be raised to a higher level of political priority and government commitment.

As a case in point, the EU adopted sanctions in 2007 banning Iranian students from receiving training in nuclear sciences in any member state, only for it to emerge later in the year that 60 Iranian nationals had been granted places at British universities to study advanced nuclear physics and engineering. This did not give the impression of an effective and joined-up counter-proliferation strategy.

We have to impart greater urgency to our efforts. Reading the great speeches of the 1950s and 1960s which led to the creation of the NPT and the IAEA, one is struck by the vividness of the threat and the extent of the terror caused by the spectre of nuclear war. John F. Kennedy, for example, spoke of a 'nuclear sword of Damocles' hanging 'by the slenderest of threads' over 'the head of every man, woman and child' in the world, 'capable of being cut at any moment by accident or miscalculation or madness'. This sense of urgency no longer pervades the debate on nuclear proliferation. I believe we need to have a galvanising moment somewhat akin to the momentum mustered by the early champions of nuclear arms control if the division and inertia of recent years is to be overcome.

We cannot afford to be complacent, and must recognise that proliferation is a moving target: the decisions of states to forgo nuclear weapons are not irrevocable, and the decision-making process of states about their security needs is a continuum. We cannot afford to switch off for a number of years while we are preoccupied in other areas.

We need to take action now to address the financing of nuclear proliferation and the nuclear black market; to create a nuclear-fuel mechanism to prevent proliferation through the fuel cycle; to establish a chain of response, enshrined in a UN Security Council resolution, to deal with countries that breach the NPT or withdraw from it; and, above all, we must redouble our efforts to prevent Iran from acquiring a nuclear weapon and shattering the NPT.

As the starting point for such a concerted strategy to revive the NPT, we should seek a common approach with the US which would combine the influence of one of the world's most powerful nuclear-weapons states with the moral authority of the UK as the nuclear-weapons state with arguably the best record in this area. An important starting point might be dialogue between the US and UK about ways to build a consensus and bring in other countries – a vital issue for the incoming president of the United States. We ought to seize the opportunity of combining a new US administration with a major British effort to push these and similar ideas. This would be a real and meaningful use of the special relationship. It is an urgent one.

Address to the IISS Global Strategic Review, Geneva, 14 September 2008

Current Conflicts: Afghanistan

Francesc Vendrell

Former European Union Special Representative for Afghanistan

Let us be frank: the current situation in Afghanistan is worse than it has been since 2001. There are military successes on the ground, but they tend to be short-lived, with the government of Afghanistan frequently failing to provide quick improvements in governance, police, justice and delivery of services, so that people in affected areas do not become attached to the government. This year, the Taliban have been able to mount both conventional and unconventional attacks, and the insurgency has geographically expanded, not only from the south to the east but also to provinces very close to Kabul and, indeed, to some parts of the north and west.

The Durand Line has become more porous than it has ever been, particularly with the Talibanisation of the Federally Administered Tribal Areas of Pakistan and parts of the North-West Frontier Province and Baluchistan.

The number of civilian casualties is rising, and even if it is true that the majority of such casualties are inflicted by the Taliban, the fact remains that these casualties and the unwillingness of the International Security Assistance Force (ISAF) and the US coalition to acknowledge them in time has created a great deal of antipathy towards the international military presence. In addition, there is increasing gang violence, linked sometimes to the Taliban, sometimes to narcotics, but also to figures in the Ministry of the Interior and the police.

On governance, we still do not have a mechanism for screening senior appointments as the international community has demanded and as was agreed at the London Conference. There has been some improvement in appointments, but currently, the perception is that appointments are made with electoral considerations in mind. There is a growing distance between the government of Afghanistan and the people, just as there tend also to be increasing differences of opinion between the government and the international community. The result of this distance between the government and the people is, I believe, that many Pashtun, even if they do not support the Taliban – and I believe that only a minority do – are sitting on the fence, waiting to see who is going to be the winner. Impunity remains, and the growth and reform of the justice system has been incredibly slow. This is, of course, one of the most difficult areas to reform in any post-conflict situation but, nonetheless, there is also a feeling that corruption is the order of the day, and this is threatening both the legitimacy and certainly the credibility of the government.

There has been virtually no progress on the disbandment of illegal armed groups, and I cite this now as one of the main reasons for where we are at the moment. On reconciliation – that is, on talks or approaches to the Taliban – there is no strategy, no framework, no red lines. We have not given any thought either to the consequences of incorporating more jihadist Islamist groups into the Afghan body politic without at the same time making any effort to assist those who want to build a secular, reformist and pluralistic society.

And finally, the country is now in the midst of a major inflation and food crisis. This is something that will need to be addressed in the very short term, otherwise it could be a very cold winter for the Afghans and a very hot winter for all of us.

How did we get where we are now? I believe the first great mistake was to convene the Bonn Conference too late. Some of us had been calling for the Bonn Conference to be convened before the Taliban fell; as it turned out, the Bonn Conference met when the Taliban had already largely disappeared and when the northern warlords, the Northern Alliance, had taken control of two-thirds of the country. So when we went to Bonn, we were faced with a fait accompli, a situation in which one group of attendees had much more power than the other group, which was mainly made up of representatives of the former king.

The second mistake was the decision by the UN, or by some people in the UN, to go for a light footprint in Afghanistan. At the time of Bonn, when the Taliban had collapsed, there was a very strong desire in Afghanistan for thorough reform: Afghans wanted to throw out not only the Taliban but the northern warlords who had, you will recall, created chaos in Afghanistan between 1992 and 1996, paving the way for the arrival of the

Taliban. But this was not to be – the UN took a low profile, there was no civil poll, and no attempt on the part of the UN to reform the police. There was no international force to receive the weapons that were to be given in as part of the disarmament, demobilisation and reintegration (DDR) process and, of course, this all began in the context of Secretary of Defense Donald Rumsfeld's abhorrence of nation-building.

The third mistake was the consignment of Afghanistan to the margins as a result of the intervention in Iraq. Iraq not only distracted the US, but the European countries as well, either because they were in favour of the intervention or because they were opposed to it – either way, the focus moved to Iraq.

The fourth mistake was the decision of the Security Council, instigated by the US, to limit ISAF to Kabul at a time, three months after 11 September 2001, when Europeans and Canadians would have been willing to send a large force to Afghanistan because we were all mesmerised by the events of 11 September. By the time that ISAF was allowed or, indeed, encouraged to move out of Kabul two years later, it was too late. By then, Europeans and Canadians were far less concerned about Afghanistan, and many of them thought that the issue of Afghanistan had virtually been solved.

Another very serious mistake has been the failure to ensure that the Afghan government has a monopoly of force. There has been no attempt, either by ISAF or by the American coalition, to help President Hamid Karzai to establish a monopoly on the means of violence. The DDR process was a voluntary process in which 60,000 dubious combatants, many of them long-retired fighters remobilised by their former commanders to reap the DDR premium, handed over mainly old weapons to sympathetic officials of the Ministry of Defence. At that time, the ministry was in the hands of Marshal Muhammad Qasim Fahim, so you had DDR weapons being handed over to a man who was more or less the country's major warlord. From the very beginning, a lot of the senior appointments went to people who had been in power in the 1990s who were corrupt, who continued to be corrupt, who had abused the population and were continuing to abuse the population, and many of whom were also linked to narcotics.

I will on this occasion pass over the opportunity to discuss something that I believe would have helped greatly, which would be to reinstate the monarchy. The monarchy would have been an antidote to the powers of the mullahs, particularly in southern Afghanistan. Another failure on our part was blindness towards Pakistan: considering that for 20 years the Pakistani authorities had been consistently supportive of the most extreme Islamist elements in Afghanistan, I think we should not have taken President Pervez

Musharraf at his word when he promised a wholesale change in Pakistani policy towards Afghanistan. The result is that only now have we come round to realising that we cannot solve the Afghan problem without also resolving the issue of the support that has until recently been given to the Taliban by Pakistan's Inter-Services Intelligence or elements within it, and without now also sorting out the problem of extremism in Pakistan itself.

We have also had a tendency to rely on personalities rather than strategic plans or institutions. We thought that we had found a miracle man, but miracle men do not exist and too much responsibility without enough power was vested in this particular person. At the same time, we have ignored the pro-democratic forces in the country, and so they remain dispersed. These represent a very large body of opinion in the urban areas, but they have found no unified voice. On reconstruction, donors have paid much attention to whether money is being spent or not, but not enough to what changes that money has brought to the people.

What is the programme that we should be following now? It is definitely not moving out of Afghanistan, as some European countries or opinion-makers might be thinking. This is not the time to leave. We are not destined to fail, but we are far from succeeding at the moment. I believe that what we need, to begin with, is a comprehensive policy towards the region. We do not have one at present. We need at least to have a policy that encompasses Afghanistan and Pakistan but, I would say, it also needs to encompass India and Iran. In the case of Iran, let me briefly say that Iran played a very positive role during the Bonn Conference. It is doubtful whether we would have reached the agreement without the assistance of the US on the one side and Iran on the other. Things have changed of course, with the failure of the moderates in Iran and the arrival of hardliners. I would describe Iranian policy now as three-pronged: a combination of support for President Karzai, the exerting of influence on Karzai to encourage him to rely on the northern warlords and commanders (because they were the traditional allies of Iran during the Taliban period) and, finally, it would not surprise me if some assistance or some relations were being developed with the Taliban. Not in order that they succeed, but in order to keep the US and UK in particular tied down in the south. What is quite clear is that a deterioration of relations with Iran would have extremely negative consequences in Afghanistan, because clearly the Iranians have a lot of means to make life far more difficult for us in the future if they so choose.

Next year will be dominated by the issue of elections. Let me say that if credible elections are not held, the situation in Afghanistan will deteriorate markedly. But we will have to ask ourselves by spring, if not earlier, whether credible elections are possible in the current security situation, in which probably 25% of the districts of Afghanistan are not accessible and this 25% happen to make up 50% of Pashtun districts. We need to do more to strengthen secular forces and to strengthen the Afghan parliament and perhaps encourage it to become more decentralised and less based in Kabul. We need also to continue to give priority to the development of central, district and provincial institutions.

Regarding our military engagement, I think we need to stay as long as the Afghan public, through its elective representatives, wants us to stay. But let us also be clear: in 2001 and 2002, we were welcomed as liberators. We are no longer welcome in this way. Our presence is now regarded as a possibly necessary evil. People do not want us to leave, because they know or believe that our departure would mean a new civil war, but we must be wary. The patience of the Afghans is not infinite, particularly not if civilian casualties continue. It is necessary to decide what policies should be followed when the Taliban are hidden in villages or other populated areas. A Status of Forces Agreement – which has now been demanded by President Karzai following the Shindand incident in which apparently 90 people were killed – is essential, and should have already happened. The Iraqi government is in the process of signing such an agreement with the US. The question of whether American forces should be detaining hundreds of Afghans without trial in Bagram and other detention centres also needs to be reviewed. Otherwise, we are setting a terrible precedent on arbitrary detention and the rule of law for any future Afghan government.

We need to concentrate more on building Afghan security forces, both the military and the police, while at the same time building up civilian institutions, primarily the judicial system, political parties, civil society and the civil service. We need to ensure that there is real improvement in local governance after there has been a military success in a given area. We must insist that the president of Afghanistan take administrative action against officials who are broadly believed to be linked to narcotics; we will not have credibility in our fight against narcotics if we do not do this. Much less evidence is of course required to dismiss an official from his post than is needed to convict him in a court of law.

We need to have a poverty-reduction and job-creation strategy, and we need to ensure that the commitments entered into by the government of Afghanistan and ourselves in London in January 2006 and in Paris in June 2008 are implemented. We should also be linking our assistance to the performance of the government, as well as ensuring that the assistance that we give makes a real difference on the ground.

I do not need to remind this audience of the importance of Afghanistan to all of us. We must continue to remember the sad experience of 11 September 2001, after we had walked away from Afghanistan for 14 years following the Soviet departure, the price we paid then and the price we continue to pay now. We also owe it to the Afghan people to ensure that they have a society where they feel that their rights are protected and where their future and their welfare is improving in reality.

Address to discussion meeting, IISS Global Strategic Review,
Geneva, 13 September 2008

European Armies: The Challenge

General David Richards

Commander-in-Chief, Land Forces, United Kingdom

Today I am going to speak candidly about some of the challenges facing
Europe as its nations struggle to ensure that the billions of euros they spend
on defence result in useable and *relevant* armed forces. Without pre-judging
what I am about to say, while there are some optimistic signs, the overall
picture is pretty bleak. Many of the reasons for this are essentially political,
rather than military, but senior soldiers must certainly accept blame too.

I will be concentrating on two questions. The first, and most important, is whether European forces are fitted for modern operations, and the
second is how we might align ambitions with reality. On the second, one
could – somewhat cynically – say that in practice, the two are well aligned,
rather dismally in some cases, in places like Afghanistan. Whether this
effort is in turn aligned with stated strategic goals is, of course, a different
question altogether.

I should emphasise that I am not going to focus today on relative
performance – the facts are readily available – but rather on establishing the strategic context in which Europe's armed forces might be used.
What deductions can be drawn from current military operations and how
might they inform our approach to the future? We need to make some
sort of judgement about the nature of future conflicts, and about what the
military's role in them might be, before we can decide whether Europe's
armies are fit for purpose.

We all know of historical instances of armies – for simplicity, I am
going to use the term 'armies' today, rather than 'armed forces' – prepar-

ing to fight the last war, rather than the next. Successful armies adapt and transform faster than their potential adversaries. In military parlance, they remain able, on a grand as well as a tactical scale, to 'seize and retain the initiative', for most soldiers the overpowering requirement for success. In the 1640s, for example, Oliver Cromwell's New Model Army defeated King Charles's initially much more impressive forces in the English Civil War because Cromwell unlocked the synergy of discipline, training, new equipment and new tactics in a manner that left the Royalists looking like amateurs – and only occasionally gifted ones. This cycle – 'pendulum' is perhaps a better term – can be found throughout history. A more recent example would be how soldiers everywhere in the 1920s struggled to understand that the era of the horse had been replaced by that of the tank.

Today, Cromwell's successors are, successfully I think, ensuring that the British Army is adapting to the challenges of conflict in Afghanistan. Self-critically, however, we should recognise that the 'transformation in contact' is still localised and small in scale; while we are certainly working towards this, we have yet to import the often subtle and certainly hi-tech methods of fighting that our soldiers now take for granted in places like Helmand into the rest of the army as it trains and equips for generic operations. Principally in response to lessons from Iraq, and as a result of a pan-Washington understanding that the US must succeed there, the US Army has done better. Its recently released FM 3-0 Operations field manual states that 'success in future conflicts will require the protracted application of all the instruments of national power – diplomatic, informational, military and economic'. It now 'equally weight[s] tasks dealing with the population – stability or civil support – with those related to offensive and defensive operations'. The key point is that the US Army is already actively structuring, equipping and training to deliver on this radical change of approach.

Having been critical of the *depth* to which we in the UK have responded to the lessons from current operations, we have done a better job on the conceptual underpinning of what it is we need to become. Though it has its critics, the UK's National Security Strategy, published in March this year, captures the essence of much of what is required for success in future conflict and is, overall, pretty good. There is a major emphasis on joint and combined operations and the military contribution is just one line of effort. The default setting is the 'comprehensive approach' to the planning, coordination and execution of operations, with other government departments fully engaged and involved throughout. The Strategy concludes that it is exceptionally unlikely that military force will be deployed in isolation to achieve solely defence-related goals and that 'the best chance of success in tackling and managing the linked challenges of instability, conflict and failed and fragile states comes from acting early, whenever possible, in a multilateral way and as part of a fully integrated approach'. We have some way to go before this fine theory is turned into effective practice but, building on our practical experience of operations in Iraq and Afghanistan, we are working towards this. Importantly, what the theory does not mean is that anything that is vaguely civilian in character can simply be left to civilians to do. In insecure and dangerous environments, often it is only the military that can achieve 'civilian effect', particularly if it is to be at the required tempo. Armies will often need to be able to deliver civilian effect – which, incidentally, means that most need still to develop it – but this must be as part of a coherent long-term political–military plan.

The net result of all of this, of course, is increasing complexity, which in turn makes more vital than ever the need for clear and authoritative chains of command. In a multinational operation, which most will be, this is the operational commander's Achilles heel. It was [US general] Omar Bradley who first observed that amateurs talk tactics, while professional talk logistics. For some time, I have been saying that professionals talk command-and-control first, then logistics, and only then tactics. At the strategic level, the same weakness exists. The absence of coherent strategic direction – at least one on which all nations in practice agree – is most damaging. In this context, I commend Sun Tzu's wise words: 'strategy without tactics is the slowest route to victory; tactics without strategy is the noise before defeat'. This is an issue to which I will return shortly, but I hope I have established in your minds that all this is about much more than equipment; command-and-control and structures being just two other important elements.

This does, however, lead me neatly on to equipment, and of course there has been a radical change in the way wars are being fought. My soldiers cannot now go back to fighting as they might have done even ten years ago. Then, it was tanks and fast jets that dominated our tactical doctrine. Today, to give you just a feel for the difference, it is expeditionary logistics, unmanned aerial vehicles, precision attack, protection, helicopters, engineers, lasers, combat-logistic patrols, chemical, biological, radiological and nuclear defence, electronic warfare, intelligence fusion, and understanding and influencing one's environment that make up a soldier's lexicon. Again, I will return to this in a moment.

In sum, operations such as those being fought in Afghanistan and Iraq show clearly that tactical, operational and strategic-level success in today's environment is beyond the abilities of a Cold War-driven military. Before I briefly wave a wet finger in the air over what the longer-term future might require of our armies, as an interesting aside, the EU is potentially hugely more powerful in the new environment than traditional collective-security organisations. In theory, through its 'Comprehensive Approach', the EU combines economic, political and military power in a single powerful (but as yet inchoate) entity, while NATO, for example, formally only wields the latter kind of power. While the defence capabilities of individual European nations must certainly be transformed on the pattern of the US military, it is only when Europe's political leaders agree on mechanisms to allow all the levers of state power to be operated cohesively in a crisis or conflict that Europe will enjoy the strategic influence its size and wealth merits. Sun Tzu's wise words on the need for strategy apply again here.

But what of the next era, assuming success in Afghanistan allows us confidently to get there? Historically, most – although not all – wars were primarily inter-state. They were driven by national interests, and success was often easy to define, normally as the military overwhelming of an opponent. Clear-cut victory was feasible, and frequently achieved. This was the approach that drove all nations' thinking on military structures, tactics and training. Defence procurement focused on equipping the force with kinetic equipment such as tanks, combat aircraft and warships. On the ground, only tactical mobility mattered, as our armies were essentially based where they were meant to fight.

Many analysts, including erstwhile chief executive of the European Defence Agency, Nick Witney, argue convincingly that, for many European countries, not much has changed. Now, these nations may not be so wrong, in principle, if one believes that traditional state-on-state warfare is what it is all about and that the types of operation that we are conducting in Afghanistan are aberrant activities. But many, myself included, believe that our generation is facing its 'horse and tank' moment, and that the way in which even state-on-state warfare will manifest itself may have changed fundamentally. Certainly, it is an issue that every nation and army needs to confront, and my own experience leads me to fear that very few really are.

Those charged with the design and equipping of armies perhaps need first to do three things. Firstly, to decide whether they believe that conflicts with dissatisfied and violent non-state actors are here for the long term, or are a historical aberration. Secondly, to decide whether they believe that, despite globalisation and mutual interdependence, state-on-state warfare remains something for which they must prepare. And thirdly – and here I think there may be some comfort to be drawn – if it is decided that our armies need to be capable of succeeding in both, do they believe that the two types of conflict would in practice look surprisingly similar, at least to those actually charged with fighting them at the tactical level? If they did appear similar, and I believe that there is a good case for thinking that they might, this would make the issue of preparing and equipping our armies much easier to agree on.

First of all, while globalisation has reduced the likelihood of inter-state warfare, it has increased the likelihood of conflict with non-state or failed-state actors. In today's environment, given the risks associated with the spread of weapons of mass destruction and the potential effects of climate change, especially in ungoverned or badly governed space in parts of Africa and the Middle East, this is something that responsible countries *must* confront more convincingly. So, point one: Europe's armies need to become much better at this type of warfare; at 'war amongst the people', as Sir Rupert Smith famously described it. In particular, how we deal with the growing disillusionment of 1.2 billion Muslims, most living in dangerously radicalised states, will be an issue that will dominate at least one generation of soldiers. Indeed, while not wishing to get into the semantics of it, perhaps the first step for us all is to accept that *this is* our generation's war, our Second World War if you like, and that it needs to be viewed and resourced accordingly.

But if I am right that non-state opponents should be our principal defence focus, inconveniently, we cannot dismiss the possibility of state-on-state warfare either. But what would such warfare actually look like? Would it really be a hot version of what people like myself spent much of our professional lives training for? I wonder. Why would China or Russia, despite the predictable clamour after [the August 2008 war in] Georgia, burden themselves with the huge costs of building armies plausibly capable of confronting us kinetically, or 'symmetrically', as it is often termed? Why would they risk everything they have achieved to attack us in this way? The presence of nuclear weapons reinforces a likely caution. If such countries really wanted to cause us major problems, and I am not that convinced that – other than conceivably for reasons relating to raw materials – even this is particularly plausible, surely they would employ other levers of state power: economic and information effects, for example. Attacks would be likely to be delivered semi-anonymously, through cyberspace or the use of proxies and guerrillas. It was, after all, the Chinese Sun

Tzu who famously reminded us that 'the acme of military skill is to defeat one's enemy without firing a shot'.

What I am suggesting is that there is a good case for believing that even state-on-state warfare would be similar to that which we will be conducting against non-state groupings. My only caveat here is that we should ensure that we do not rush headlong into scrapping all our tanks, to the point that traditional mass-armoured operations become an attractive asymmetric option to a potential enemy. However, the presence of the residual armoured forces needed to ensure tactical-level dominance in counter-insurgency operations, plus air power and nuclear weapons – which, though a baleful presence, would in this context be beneficial – will remain a powerful deterrent against any such temptation.

If I am right, the golden lining of all this is that European armies can make virtue of necessity by focusing on essentially one type of conflict. Whether one is fighting non-state actors in Afghanistan or proxies of a disgruntled major power there or somewhere else, the skill sets and weapon systems required will look usefully similar. In either case, as in Iraq and Afghanistan today, delivering success will need boots on the ground, and lots of them. In the Cold War, our armies were considerably larger than they are now, and designed primarily to conduct short-duration conventional war-fighting operations. In such operations, one could compensate for what would historically be viewed as a shortage of troops with huge firepower. If we are serious about succeeding with acceptable casualties and, in the case of somewhere like Afghanistan, in a time frame that meets the host nation's expectations as well as those of our own domestic public opinion, we need to look again at the number of soldiers we have to fight future wars, whether state or non-state in nature. It is a false economy to drip-feed troops into these conflicts. The old adage 'clout don't dribble' has much to commend it, and is certainly the reason why Britain was successful in Sierra Leone in 2000. Were any of us surprised by the success of the US surge in Iraq? It succeeded for the same reason *Operation Motorman* did in Belfast in 1972. While there were other ingredients, a key element of the formula was that we got the force ratios right. In wars amongst the people, if you are using a lot of firepower, you are almost certainly losing. I am reminded of an experienced British colonial general who, when asked by a brigadier if he could have a couple of battalions to resolve a problem in Burma, famously told him, 'No, but you can have a division, because that's what you'll need.'

So, finally, to some detail to help answer the two questions I posed at the start: are European armies fitted for modern operations and if not, how might we align ambitions to reality, hopefully as that reality develops? You are all capable of making up your own minds on these issues, but I suspect that if there was a show of hands, the vast majority here would say that all is not well. In this area, most of our armies look strikingly like they did at the end of the Cold War. Tanks may, in some cases, be smarter, but across the board these forces are not capable of exploiting the synergies to be gained from technology, let alone of displaying the skills needed to manage the peace that might follow any such modern or future conflict. And Bradley would turn in his grave over the state of their logistics.

The EU has itself undertaken an analysis of its capabilities against a number of scenarios and the results have been captured in a so-called Progress Catalogue. This assesses operational risk and concludes that there are a number of critical shortfalls, especially in the fields of force protection – in particular, ballistic protection from improvised explosive devices and rocket-propelled grenades – ISTAR,* inter-theatre and intra-theatre lift. And the EU analysis was being gentle on itself. The assessments were based on the so-called 'Petersberg tasks' and – certainly when compared to current practice in Iraq or Afghanistan – they do not capture the totality of the shortfall. The lack of deployable helicopters is especially critical. European nations between them reportedly possess 1,437 helicopters. Five hundred and fifty-one are classed as 'NATO deployable', although only 44 could be identified as potentially meeting the operational requirements of Afghanistan in the 2006 NATO Defence Planning Questionnaire. This huge discrepancy is of course due to the fact that a fleet of helicopters only becomes a proper operational capability when one rigorously addresses training and logistic needs, to pick on only two necessary elements.

Perhaps all this is not surprising, given EU defence expenditure and, in particular, the manner in which the budget is being used. EU states on average only spend 1.78% of GDP on defence. The US figure is about 4.7%. This is a fairly binary means of comparison, but more significantly, the US spends three times as much per soldier as the EU (€350,000 versus €103,000). Also, personnel costs represent only 20% of the US defence budget, compared to a 55% average in the EU. I am not a statistician, and I accept that there is an element of fixed cost in this, but my instinct tells me that EU forces need to drive down this figure by rebalancing expenditure more efficiently. The US, it seems, gets more for its money. This becomes more apparent when you consider the deployability figures for

---

*   Intelligence, surveillance, target acquisition and reconnaissance.

EU member states. Viewing the number of deployed troops as a percentage of total military personnel, only six nations – the UK, Estonia, the Netherlands, Ireland, Sweden and Germany – exceed the 5% average for Europe. The remaining member states are below this figure. Compared with the US figure of 14%, this is pretty risible.

So what do we need to do? First and foremost, our armies all need to be able to fight, exploiting new technologies synergistically. They also need to be of the right size to succeed in stability operations, operations that may not be such a burden when they are shared with other, similarly capable, armies. And, crucially, they need to understand and exploit the tools of information superiority. There is more, but let me now focus on one other ill-understood spectre at this feast, which is the issue of interoperability. Modern operations are characterised by a multinational and multi-agency approach that places a premium on interoperability. In an ideal world, we would all be fully interoperable and, however difficult it is to attain, that should certainly be our goal. NATO's Airborne Early Warning and Control Force is a good example of what can be achieved, in its case principally through the pooling of equipment. Interoperability, though, is not just limited to equipment. It includes things that should be more easily in our gift; for example, training, tactics, techniques and procedures. One common complaint that US forces make when supporting the British alone is that, rather typically, there is not one standard set of standard operating procedures. This causes friction. We need to drive down self-imposed friction – the enemy adds enough as it is!

Another variation on this key theme, and I have emphasised the critical importance of command-and-control in the round, is our collective inability to communicate effectively within and between headquarters. This is not just due to equipment incompatibility. Virtually every nation's security regime and architectures is a significant hindrance to operational command. Our priority ought to be to be able to share information multinationally, rather than protecting it nationally. Yet virtually every nation favours the latter approach. This results in our procuring national communications and information systems to train on, then using a completely different set of command systems in the coalition context on operations. For example, in Iraq, there is the INet system, and in Afghanistan the ISAF WAN system. This is neither efficient nor effective: it places additional strain on both the communications-and-information-systems provider and the user, and it can often negate the point of holding forces at high readiness. The effect in theatre is to limit operational commanders' ability to manage information risk. I hope you can see why I said earlier that today's true professionals place such emphasis on command-and-control. Interestingly, in 1999, even a small power such as Australia, having thought these issues through a bit, was able to have a command-and-control solution ready on day one for countries such as the UK when we deployed with it on the INTERFET operation in East Timor. Nearly ten years on, we would not be readily able to do the same.

On a more optimistic note, there is progress. The EU battlegroup concept looks promising. There are fifteen battlegroups, and all but five are composed of two or more nations. However, there are limitations in their capability and use, and they rely heavily on strategic enablers, an area in which we currently have significant capability shortfalls. But from small beginnings come great things. The key is for the battlegroups to be able to fight, and for this they need the type of modern equipment that is being used in operational theatres now. If we subscribe to this approach, in time it can be extended across the rest of the EU's armies. And in the meantime, we must not dismiss the potential effect of a battlegroup-sized intervention force. *Operation Palliser*, the UK's intervention in Sierra Leone in 2000, is not a bad exemplar of a small-scale operation.

But, to return to where I started, for even this to succeed, political cohesion is vital. *Operation Palliser* was a single-nation operation and, while not perfect in this respect, it was probably as coherent as one can get. If we cannot achieve in multinational operations that unity of command considered by Clausewitz and others to be a *sine qua non* of strategic success, we must at least achieve genuine unity of effort. From my own experience in Afghanistan, I know that the importance of this issue is not well understood. We must do better. As our guide, I commend a clear answer to the old military adage, 'who is responsible to whom for what?'. Too often, all is very murky, and this leads inevitably to too much discussion and too little effective, timely action.

In sum, Europe's armies, including my own, have much to do. Firstly, we need to agree on the essential nature of future conflict and, as you have heard, I believe that there are some synergies to be had here. Once agreed, we must vigorously restructure and re-equip accordingly. Most importantly, though, we must succeed in Afghanistan. If we do not, we will not have the moral authority or confidence needed to succeed elsewhere in the future.

From a soldier's perspective, we cannot do all this without clear political direction. It is now our political masters who must be engaged in this key debate, much more authoritatively assisted by their generals. If this issue, our horse-and-tank moment, is not gripped, European armed forces will continue to try, with hopelessly inadequate resources, to be all things to all conflicts and fail to succeed properly at anything. The risks of such an approach are now just too serious for this any longer to be an acceptable course, if it ever has been.

Address to the IISS Global Strategic Review, Geneva, 14 September 2008

Europe and Conflict Resolution: Isolated or Engaged?

Lieutenant-General Karl Eikenberry

Deputy Chairman, Military Committee, NATO

I have been asked to contribute some thoughts to this panel discussion on the question 'Europe and Conflict Resolution: Isolated or Engaged?'. Let me focus on the security side of the equation, on so-called 'hard power'. I would like to emphasise before I begin that I am speaking here as an individual, and not as a representative of an institution. I would like also to mention that, after two tours of duty in Afghanistan serving in command of and side-by-side with European soldiers, sailors, airmen and marines, I have been enormously impressed by the courage, dedication and initiative displayed by these European forces.

What I would like to do is to offer two main points for discussion. The first is a critique of EU security and defence policy and the second, perhaps of more interest to this group, is some speculation on areas in which NATO and the EU could seek greater degrees of collaboration, cooperation and synergy, which, I believe, would in the long run work to the benefit of the European Security and Defence Policy (ESDP).

Let me begin with the critique of EU security and defence policy. There are three areas that I would like to cover here: strategy, levels of ambition and operations. First, let us talk about the EU security and defence strategy. It is not clear to me that Europe has a meaningful, coherent strategy that goes beyond its borders. There is clearly an overwhelming preference within Europe for soft power; it is entirely unclear what role is to be played by hard power. European security documents clearly reflect the fact that Europe now sees its security as going beyond its boundaries, but it is not at all evident that this recognition has yet translated into firm security policies. Some examples: Europe's strategy does not clearly articulate its regional priorities, nor does it even properly address what its responses to recognised transnational threats should be. To cite one specific example here – since 2003, the EU has conducted some 20 operations, some of which are ongoing. Many of these operations have been successful. Of the 20, five have been conducted in the Democratic Republic of the Congo (DRC) – again, successful operations, but some have been episodic and without clear strategic end-states. I do not mean at all to criticise the operations that have taken place in the DRC. The DRC needs security, and the EU through its conduct of operations there has exported security. There has clearly been value added. My only point is to ask, in terms of an overarching grand strategy for the EU, of 20 operations, why five in the Congo? What is the strategic end-state and what are the goals and objectives being sought there? It is, as they say, difficult to reach a destination if you do not know where you are going. Regarding the EU's core identity on the issue of security, the question is, is the EU Europe-focused, or does it have a truly global ambition on security? If it has a global ambition, then interest and priorities need clear articulation.

The second area is levels of ambition. The EU has clear force constructs that have been established for some years, a headline goal of 60,000 forces in a state of readiness for deployment. More recently, French President Nicolas Sarkozy has articulated a thoughtful approach towards defining an array of scenarios and contingencies from which force constructs and sets of capabilities can be obtained. But let us go beyond these constructs and examine the realities of current capabilities, that is, the ability and the will to deliver capabilities and forces.

There are two measures to be looked at: first, overall levels of defence effort. Today, a quarter of global defence spending is represented by the EU; €200 billion. But it is not clear that its investments are the right investments – currently, less than 30% of Europe's forces are expeditionary, that is, less than 30% of the force structure can be used outside Europe. There is still within Europe the notion of going it alone, and there are still significant redundancies in the areas of the development of capabilities and the fielding of forces. I have seen this first hand in Afghanistan, where we have many great European forces that are serving in an expeditionary environment, but all with unique logistics requirements, because the equipment is not compatible, not interoperable. Thus we have many, many logistics streams coming from various European countries. So the issue is not necessarily the amount of money being spent, rather *how* the money is being spent, which leads to the second question: is Europe taking defence modernisation seriously?

Some indicators: on average, European armed forces currently spend 55% of the budget on personnel. By way of comparison, in the US armed forces, 20% of the budget is spent on personnel. On average, European nations are spending 19% of their defence budgets on procurement and research and development. The US is spending 29%. Defence investment per soldier is a very important indicator of seriousness of purpose, especially in the context of making serious investments in soldiers and formations to permit them to operate in very difficult expeditionary environments outside our borders. The US spends an average of €100,000 per soldier. Of the EU countries, only two spend more than €30,000 per soldier and only five spend more than €20,000.

Sixty-four capability objectives were set as part of Europe's 1999 Helsinki headline goals. In 2006, taking stock of progress in relation to the goals, 12 of those 64 capability objectives had been successfully achieved – and that is being somewhat generous with the definition of success. Over 50 had not been achieved. If we look at those not achieved, we come back to expeditionary capabilities – helicopters, intelligence, air-to-air refuelling and command-and-control, I could go on. Finally, and very pointedly, I must pose this question: in the year 2008, what is the relative status or prestige of defence ministers within the cabinets of various European countries today, at least relative to their position at the height of the Cold War? This, too, is an indicator of seriousness of purpose.

There have been some very important successes that the EU has achieved, of which the European battlegroup concept is one. There have been some overwhelming successes in particular areas of the field of European armaments and materiel. And there have also been some very noteworthy successes achieved in the area of limited multinational cooperation.

But I leave this domain of levels of ambition with two questions. Has there been too great a disarmament by all of us after the Cold War? And has the success of the EU economically and politically, which has had consequences for the relevance of the nation-state, led to a collective-action security problem that exists within NATO? More specifically, is an attack on one European capital perceived within Europe as an attack on all capitals?

The third and final area of my critique is an assessment of EU-led operations. As I said earlier, since 2003, some 20 EU operations have been conducted. Only five of the 20 have involved more than 1,000 deployed personnel. Nine have involved fewer than 100. So we should be clear about scales of effort. Secondly, only a very small percentage of Europe's military personnel has been or is currently deployed on EU operations. The figure currently stands at around 6,000, roughly a third of 1%. Third point: force generation remains extraordinarily difficult for Europe, and this is exacerbated by a very perverse funding mechanism known as 'costs lie where they fall'. What is 'costs lie where they fall'? Essentially, you pay as you go for operations, a huge disincentive against seriously engaging in an expeditionary operation.

The EU correctly says that it has an advantage in delivering the comprehensive approach. I have seen this at work first-hand, in the Balkans and Afghanistan. It is indeed impressive, but equally, when Europe talks about its comparative advantage in the comprehensive approach, we must also critique how Europe has done on developing to take advantage of its strengths in this area. How much progress has it made in developing the truly expeditionary, non-military capability essential to delivering the comprehensive approach in expeditionary environments?

Secondly, if Europe has an advantage in the comprehensive approach, why does the EU compartmentalise its military and civilian sides? Why does it not have a seamless, integrated command-and-control that would allow it to actually apply the comprehensive approach that it needs if it really aspires to be a global player in the security domain?

Now let me turn to my second topic: opportunities for the EU and NATO to collaborate and cooperate in ways that will enable Europe and the ESDP to become a much more global player, capable of delivering comprehensive security. Five observations here: NATO's problems are very much the same as the EU's, only, I suppose, on a grander scale. Force generation remains a very serious problem for NATO. Inefficient business practices cause difficulties – we in NATO also have the 'costs lie where they fall' practice, a disincentive to participating in expeditionary operations. We lack expeditionary capabilities, and we have antiquated doctrine that needs to be updated. As our secretary-general is fond of saying, a *Puma* helicopter flying in Afghanistan with NATO markings looks like a NATO helicopter flying in Chad with EU markings, which looks like a *Puma* helicopter flying in Lebanon with a UN logo. In other words, these are common problems that we all face together. Our solutions must be collaborative, and our approaches complementary.

My second point is that, currently, all our forces – America's, Canada's, Europe's – are stretched. We must find ways to share our forces. It makes no sense to have separate sets of forces within the EU and NATO set aside for reserves and standby. Experience in the Balkans has shown a very promising way forward, with collaboration there between the EU forces in Bosnia-Herzegovina and Kosovo forces under NATO command. But we do have to move beyond the notion that 'standardising' our forces constitutes success; we must share our forces.

Third point: beyond forces and capabilities, we must also look at so-called enablers, at other support agencies, and find ways to more broadly share these as well. Let me give some examples. The NATO Maintenance and Supply Agency is currently doing superb contracting work in Afghanistan and the NATO Communications and Information Systems Services Agency is a very effective agency that provides the communications backbone for NATO expeditionary forces and for our infrastructure. The NATO Consultation, Command and Control Agency does superb work in the area of force planning and modelling. Why is it that these kinds of capability are for NATO only, why can they not be shared with the EU? We currently have one good example of such sharing, a movement-control centre in Eindhoven that is shared by the EU and NATO. We found a way to do this seamlessly, but I believe that we need to be more ambitious.

My fourth point is that there is a need for strategic dialogue between NATO and the EU. We have long discussions on the issues I am discussing now, about the need to pool and share resources in order to eliminate redundancies and achieve efficiencies. But if we are strategically redundant, if we are strategically competitive with one another, where does all this debate about tactics and organisation and forces ultimately lead us? What are our respective zones of interest? What are our comparative advantages? What are our presumed respective levels of ambition?

So to my fifth and final point, speaking, again, very much as an individual: on the issue of collaboration between NATO and the EU, the ball may be very much in the EU's court. Unlike in the 1990s, today the US's door is wide open for NATO–EU collaboration in the security domain; it appears wide open for a united EU, a united Europe, to walk through. The challenge, I believe, is for Europe to define its defence identity and its strategic ways, means and ends and, very importantly, to address forthrightly the very contentious political issues that prevent real progress in this area.

Strategic Survey 2008 Launch Address, IISS, London, 18 September 2008

John Chipman
Director-General and Chief Executive, IISS

This *Strategic Survey* went to press in late July, just before the Russian–Georgian war that appeared to change importantly East–West relations. *Strategic Survey* did not predict this war, though its assessment of the instability in the Caucasus laid out the reasons why it was possible, and its analysis of the deteriorating state of Western–Russian relations anticipated the anger that the Russians would display towards the perceived attempt by Georgia to take advantage of its close relationship to the West to settle the frozen conflicts in its favour.

The Russia–Georgia crisis, as I will argue in a moment, does not usher in a new Cold War. The crisis should invite a more considered strategic analysis by the West and NATO of policy towards the East that takes into proper account wider strategic interests and is more specific about what kind of Russian activity it is necessary to deter or prevent. In particular, NATO enlargement policy should be reaffirmed as necessary if it is in the service of NATO strategic interests, a means to an end, not an institutional priority in itself. NATO must not transform its expansion policy into a game of Russian roulette. A more immediate priority than planning further enlargement is to provide appropriate strategic reassurance to existing members. A medium-term need is to calculate how best to engage in the Caucasus with Ukraine and with other areas in Russia's neighbourhood. The approach should be regional, not just country-specific. Where there are still frozen conflicts, diplomatic discussions must be rekindled. In time, NATO and Western countries need to sort out exactly what interests are worth defending and in what manner, and on what issues it may still be possible to collaborate with Russia in order to induce more congenial behaviour in other areas. A strategic approach to Russia must acknowledge, without necessarily accepting, the nature of Russia today and focus Western influence and leverage where it most matters. Western leaders have called for an audit of EU–Russian relations; they may also want to make an audit of what their most important interests are with Russia in current circumstances.

Overview

During the past year, the leaders of the major powers were, in general, mostly preoccupied by domestic and economic developments: the US with its presidential election, China with the Olympic Games, Russia with a leadership shuffle. The inward focus of many countries was partly a response to the effects of the triple shock in the markets for credit, oil and food.

As a result, regional actors were able to assume larger conflict-resolution roles for themselves. Turkey began playing a role in facilitating possible peace talks between Israel and Syria. Qatar played a crucial role in mediating between Lebanese groups to allow the accession of the new president of Lebanon. South Africa persisted in its regional mediation to create a power-sharing agreement in Zimbabwe. Qatar's and South Africa's diplomatic roles were not always applauded in the West. The feeling in both cases was that the agreements negotiated went too much with the grain of local conditions, the first by granting too much formal power to Hizbullah within the Lebanese system, the second by according too much residual power to President Robert Mugabe. Working too much with the grain of local and international conditions strikes some people as defeatist. Occasionally, it is the technique that avoids the worst outcomes. These are the sorts of stopgap measures that are often needed when the bigger diplomatic powers are distracted. A more egalitarian international diplomatic order may not openly be achievable at the UN Security Council, but in practice it is, for better or for worse, being established on the ground.

More widely, the year saw grey returning as the main colour on the diplomatic palette, pushing the presumed certainties of black and white to the sidelines. Diplomatic compromise, moderation of strategic objectives and acknowledgement of practical power balances were the general themes. The idealistic and entrepreneurial mode of Western foreign policy is over. How idealism and realpolitik will intermingle in the future will hugely depend on the personality of the future US president. But there is an abiding sense that the age of ambitious democratisation agendas and regional strategic makeovers is behind us.

Iranian and North Korean proliferation issues

The diplomatic efforts to stem the nuclear-proliferation challenges posed by Iran and North Korea are both deadlocked. In defiance of four Security Council resolutions, Iran continues to expand its uranium-enrichment programme, with around 4,000 centrifuges now installed at Natanz and operating fairly well. Iran also continues to resist efforts by the International Atomic Energy Agency to probe allegations of past design work on nuclear weapons, including foreign help with experiments on a detonator suitable for an implosion-type weapon.

In June, Iran was presented with a repackaged incentives proposal, which included a 'double freeze' on both additional centrifuges and additional sanctions as a face-saving way to start negotiations on a long-term solution. In July, the US floated a plan to post consular officers to Tehran, and sent its third-ranking diplomat to Geneva for preliminary discussions with Iran led by EU foreign-policy chief Javier Solana. Iran responded with positive words but no expressed willingness to limit its nuclear programme. Frustrated by the lack of a substantive reply, the US and its allies vowed to pursue a new sanctions resolution in the Security Council.

The prospects for significantly tougher UN sanctions were never strong, however, and are even less so in the aftermath of the Georgia crisis. Pressure on Iran will grow, but largely outside the auspices of the UN. The next year could see Iran reaching the kind of threshold capability that would seriously worry Israel and rekindle talk of potential military action.

It will take North Korea less than one year to undo the steps that up until August it was taking to disable its declared nuclear facilities. Pyongyang began the reversal when Washington refused to finally remove North Korea from the list of state sponsors of terrorism and the US Trading with the Enemy Act. The US demanded that North Korea first agree to a process for verifying the declaration it had provided about its plutonium programme. Uncertainty about the health of North Korean leader Kim Jong Il solidifies the stalemate that is likely to continue at least until a new US president takes office.

Iraq, Afghanistan and Pakistan

The handing over of the command of US forces in Iraq this week brings to a close a very successful tour of duty for General David Petraeus. Petraeus presided over a decline in civil strife that saw the monthly tally of violent deaths fall from its peak of 3,500 Iraqi civilians killed in January 2007 to 550 in July 2008. Violence has reduced in Anbar province, once the epicentre of the insurgency, to such an extent that responsibility for the province's security could be handed over to the Iraqi Army and police force at the beginning of September. However, both Petraeus and his successor General Ray Odierno have been very cautious about the sustainability of these security gains.

The reasons for this pessimism are to be found in the lack of comparable progress in Iraqi politics. The position of Prime Minister Nuri al-Maliki has certainly strengthened over 2008, and his popularity increased after he deployed the army to both Basra and Mosul, Iraq's second- and third-largest cities, with a subsequent increase in security. However, Maliki's growing power and confidence have not been matched by a growth in his support in Iraq's parliament, the Council of Representatives. Maliki's continued rule is still dependent on a small but fractious coalition of two Shia Islamist parties and the two Kurdish parties. Crucial legislation needed to distribute Iraq's oil revenues and manage overdue provincial elections remains stuck in the parliament, hindered by the seeming inability of legislators and their party bosses to reach agreement on a number of key issues.

Overall, there has been significant progress in Iraq during 2008. But for this to become irreversible, Iraq's ruling elite needs to find a way to compromise on political and revenue issues without resorting to extra-parliamentary violence. Successful provincial and national elections, both likely to take place in 2009, will determine whether gains can be sustained.

In the meantime, attention is migrating powerfully towards Afghanistan, where the many challenges in the country are compounded by the worsening situation in Pakistan's Federally Administered Tribal Areas (FATA). New Pakistani President Asif Ali Zardari's top priority is to fight terrorism and Islamist militancy in the tribal areas bordering Afghanistan. But with over 110,000 troops deployed in the FATA, the Pakistani Army remains unable or unwilling to effectively counter the resurgent Taliban. With the Taliban controlling large swathes of the tribal areas and an increase in cross-border attacks on Coalition forces in Afghanistan, the US is now inclined to attack these 'safe havens' in an attempt to defeat the Taliban. An increase in US strikes by missile-armed unmanned aircraft, and the first ground assault by Coalition Special Forces in the tribal areas during Ramadan on 3 September, resulted in public outrage in Pakistan. In a rare public statement, Pakistan's army chief, General Ashfaq Kayani, condemned these attacks and stated that the country would be defended 'at all cost'.

Zardari's major challenge will be to gain the trust of the army and build a consensus against terrorism and Islamist extremism among the political establishment. To pursue the campaign on terror, he will need to balance the conflicting interests of growing US pressure for military strikes in the tribal areas with the Pakistani Army's decreasing tolerance for such attacks. And, in order to reduce public opposition to such a policy, he needs to build bridges with the major opposition political parties. Most importantly, Zardari will need to ensure that domestic political turbulence, heightened by the growing economic crisis, does not place his government at risk from the army.

Russia and Georgia: strategic implications

The balance of evidence at present suggests that Georgia started the August war, having amassed troops on the border with South Ossetia on the morning of 7 August, and launching attacks on the South Ossetian capital Tskhinvali before Russian tanks passed through the Roki Tunnel. Precise timelines may not be firmly established before the results of inquiries demanded by numerous bodies, including the US Congress. But Bush administration officials freely acknowledge that they warned Georgia in forceful terms against initiating military action in South Ossetia, and feel that that advice was ignored. Georgia's apparent decision openly to reject the demands of its US patron not to seek to recover South Ossetia by force was clearly irresponsible. It raises the legitimate question of whether Georgia, as an aspirant member of a Western military alliance system, would be a responsible member of that grouping if it were to fail to act in multilateral consultation with its supporters.

Russia's reaction to the Georgian effort to place the frozen conflict of South Ossetia in a military microwave was disproportionately strong. The spread of its army through Georgia proper was unjustified by any immediate requirement to protect the South Ossetians on whose behalf Moscow claims to have acted. The establishment of multiple checkpoints all around Georgia was excessive. The destruction of parts of Georgia's infrastructure was vindictive. The decision quickly to recognise South Ossetia and Abkhazia had a pre-emptive quality to it, and has already shown itself to have placed a diplomatic burden on Russia, especially in light of the near-universal condemnation of the move.

But the Russians were not aiming, as commentators and the president of Georgia later claimed, to change the map of post-war Europe.

Russia's actions in Georgia, aggressive as they were, cannot be read as the European equivalent of Saddam Hussein's attempt to overrun Kuwait in August 1990. What Moscow did intend was to draw a line at the extension of the Western sphere of strategic influence further eastwards. The West must decide whether, given its wider global agenda and the specific need for collaboration with Russia over such issues as Afghanistan and Iran, locking horns with Russia over the Caucasus is necessary.

As a practical matter, there is a high risk that the momentum of NATO enlargement policy will divide the West. Despite the fact that 20% of Georgia's territory has been lost, the United States will probably argue for continuing on the path towards eventual membership. It will do the same for Ukraine, even though the population of that country and its divided leadership is ambivalent about, if not in the majority opposed to, NATO membership. Europeans have a strong case to argue that it is in NATO's strategic interest to pause its enlargement policy. While Russia has no veto on NATO membership, mere possession of a perceived threat is equally no automatic ticket to entry. Europe will want to invite the US to think strategically, not nostalgically, about the weight it wishes to attach to NATO enlargement in its regional policy. Georgia has weakened its case for NATO membership. It openly defied its main strategic patron, the US, by seeking to recover its lost territories, took on a declared Russian interest without the ability to do so alone, and then called on the West to sort out the mess it had created. Small allies pay a tax to larger strategic guarantors. In return for the promise of assistance, they must at least consult them.

NATO has set up commissions with Ukraine and Georgia, and these must be allowed to work. Meanwhile, the West must think through what its true strategic interests are in the EU–NATO–Russia neighbourhood. Dealing with Russia in the current circumstances is extremely difficult. It wants to assert its interests widely with greater force. It sometimes makes decisions based more on pique and anger than on strategic calculus and self-interest. Russia has made its bad temper almost an instrument of its foreign policy. Scowling at every affront to its status, it has revived the doctrine that 'the enemy of my enemy is my friend' as a guide for its diplomacy. But the West must not reply to this defiant mood with a form of strategic autism, advancing its interests blind to the emotional response that this can elicit from the Russian leadership.

A bit of old-fashioned sangfroid is called for in these unfortunately quite old-fashioned strategic times. Russia is isolated even within its own declared sphere of influence. None of its partners in the Shanghai

Cooperation Organisation have recognised Abkhazia and South Ossetia. China is appalled by Russia's validation of secessionist politics.

The West must develop a strategy that fills out the content of the policy of hard-headed engagement that is sometimes advertised. This means defining interests in the region and with Russia in a more clear-headed manner, distinguishing between the necessary and the desirable. It has been some time since the West developed a truly specific Russia policy; perhaps it was not thought necessary in the immediate post-Cold War period: it is now.

Conclusion

The events of August 2008 do not signify fresh steps towards a new Cold War because neither side wants one, and the stakes are too low to warrant one. They do mark the distinct end of the romantic phase of the post-Cold War order. Russia is not yet the liberal democratic power some both within and outside Russia wished for. But, like everyone else, Russia is subject to those forces of globalisation that could place a check on its progress. The most powerful remark about Russia's actions in Georgia was not made by the EU or NATO, but by the markets, wiping so much value off Russian stocks and effectively marking up Russian risk.

The next few months will see many preoccupied with the outcome of the US election. However much America's individual share of global power has been in relative decline, it remains the case that it is the 'swing' geopolitical player, the one that by its action or inaction can have the most impact on the comity of nations and the stability of the international system as a whole. But we are now entering an era in which international diplomatic activity will be more plural. America is unable now to shape the international agenda alone, and needs international partners. Those prospective partners, in Europe, the Middle East, Asia and elsewhere, need to be more assertive in developing initiatives that the US can comfortably join, rather than merely reacting to proposals that may come from Washington. The quality of those initiatives will determine whether the post-unipolar moment will be more or less good for international peace and security.

Address to the IISS Global Strategic Review, Geneva, 13 September 2008

The War in the Caucasus: Causes and Strategic Implications

Oksana Antonenko

Senior Fellow for Russia and Eurasia, IISS

It is rather difficult for me to address this issue and to talk about the current conflict in the Caucasus. There are three reasons for this. One is that, for two and a half years, I have been mediating the informal 'track-one-and-a-half' Georgian–Ossetian dialogue process, which was the only initiative of the past ten years to bring together senior Georgian and South Ossetian officials in a purely bilateral format to discuss the prospects for conflict resolution. I saw with my own eyes what could have been done just three years ago to genuinely encourage the conflict-resolution process and to avoid arriving at the situation that we are in at the moment. I feel sorry that this and other opportunities to prevent what happened on 7 August were missed.

My second reason for feeling uneasy talking about the current situation is because I lived through the Cold War in the Soviet Union, and I am upset by how easily in the current crisis we have become engaged in an extremely unproductive discussion about a 'new Cold War'. To me, it is very clear that what we have today has nothing at all to do with the Cold War, and I think that this rhetoric and this thinking – which has unfortunately been frequently found both in the media and in the statements of officials on all sides – is extremely unhelpful to understanding how we move towards genuine resolution of the current crisis.

The third reason is that, regrettably, in the way in which it has been reported so differently by the Western and Russian medias, this has been a very classic conflict. Being able to observe the differences and to give interviews to both sides, I can see the extent to which there are completely opposing perceptions of what has happened and what is going on now. It is very difficult to bridge this gap in understanding, but I will attempt to do so.

I believe that the crisis has progressed through three stages. The first stage – which lies at the core of the problem – is the inter-ethnic conflict between Georgians and Ossetians, which has a very long history, stretching over decades. In the second stage, Russia's intervention transformed this conflict into the Georgian–Russian conflict that is now a source of great anxiety for many countries along Russia's borders. Now, at the third stage, I think we have a rather new type of conflict, which is this diplomatic confrontation, or whatever we wish to call it, between Russia and the West. We must address the current crisis at all three of these levels.

The key challenges to address now are the following. First, we need to think about how Russia and the West can move from the current crisis to once again be able to address in a positive manner the key international issues that we face today, such as non-proliferation, conflict resolution and arms control. We are in a situation now in which both Russia and the West are engaged, not so much in a zero-sum game but in a negative-sum one, and I believe that if we do not find a way out of this dynamic, serious and vital interests will be affected on both sides.

The second point that we need to address is the extent to which events in the Caucasus, Russia's unilateral intervention in particular, are part of a pattern of unilateral intervention, which also comprises the intervention in the Balkans and the intervention in Iraq, and how we might give back to international institutions such as the United Nations and others the authority to deal with any future crises.

The third issue that we need to think about is how to reassure countries such as Ukraine and others in the former Soviet Union, which feel that their security has been weakened. These countries are looking for more guarantees, new engagement from the international community to ensure that their security is not undermined in the future.

The fourth issue, which is extremely important, is how to address the wider insecurity and instability that is going to be with us in the Caucasus for many years to come. It is crucial to deal with this issue, because not only is the Caucasus a pivotal region geographically, it also plays a very important role in relation both to Europe's energy-security agenda and, of course, to the prospects for Central Asia's economic development, as well as its own.

With all this in mind, I would like to make a further few points. First, I would like to offer my view of what actually happened. There are so many different interpretations of events that it is very important to try to understand what happened in this war. I would also like to consider the question of whether this crisis could have been prevented, and what might have been the key failures of the international community in dealing with it. I would like too to offer some thoughts about where we go from here and about the key implications of the crisis that will need to be addressed.

First, then: what happened? Having been engaged on the ground in these conflict regions for many years, it is my view that this escalation was entirely predictable; it was not in the least a surprise development. I think that it was quite clear that, sooner or later, conflicts that had been 'frozen' for more than fifteen years would escalate. I believe that the international community bears substantial responsibility for ignoring these conflicts for too long, and that the assumption that conflicts such as the one in South Ossetia could have been frozen indefinitely was unjustified, as of course has now turned out to be the case.

In my view, there is no doubt that the current crisis began on 7 August, when Georgia attacked South Ossetia. Clearly, the crisis had been building up for a number of weeks and months, but the current crisis can be dated from roughly 11pm on 7 August. I find it striking that the international response to this development did not come until several days later. I was among a group of experts who met Prime Minister Vladimir Putin the day before yesterday, and I found what he said on this very interesting. As his comments were on the record, I feel I can share some of his points with you. Putin said that at 10am Beijing time, several hours after the attack had begun, he contacted US President George Bush and told him that there was a major problem in the Caucasus. According to Putin, Bush responded by saying that nobody wanted a war and, as Putin understood it, promised to do something to deal with the problem. Putin then told us that when the two met at the opening ceremony of the Olympic Games more than nine hours later, he spoke to Bush once again and asked him what he had done to deal with the problem, and it appeared to him that nothing had been done.

I think that this was the biggest shock for Putin, the sense that there was no real willingness on the part of the international community to look at what was going on and understand its implications. By no means do I wish to blame the US for the crisis. That would not be fair, but I think that what is clear is that the fact that we waited for hours and days for the UN and the international community to intervene in the crisis did create a veneer of legitimacy – and I want to emphasise that it was a veneer – for Russia's intervention.

It is also important to point out that the Georgian attack on 7 August involved the overwhelming and indiscriminate use of force against civilians in Tskhinvali. I believe that this attack was unjustifiable. It is important too to remember that not only civilians but also Russian peacekeepers were killed in the attack, which of course furnished the pretext for Russia's intervention in the absence of international reaction. At the same time, Russia was clearly following a much wider agenda by intervening in South Ossetia, and by going too far in its intervention and occupying and bombing parts of 'Georgia proper', it certainly lifted the veneer of legitimacy, prompting what was, in my view, a justified reaction from the international community when it described Russia's actions as 'completely unacceptable'.

The intervention of President Nicolas Sarkozy has been very welcome. Unfortunately, however, the agreement on the ceasefire contained so many ambiguities that it was difficult to implement in a way that would have brought a quick and decisive end to the initial stage of the conflict.

The Russian recognition of Abkhazia and South Ossetia was, I believe, predictable, and should not have come as a surprise given that for many months, Russia had been warning that any Georgian action in Abkhazia or South Ossetia would mean the end of ambiguity over their status and a likely Russian recognition. At the same time, I believe that to recognise Abkhazia and South Ossetia in the way that it has done has been the most important strategic mistake that Russia has made. The recognition was completely unilateral, without any attempt being made to abide by international law, follow any procedure, be it through the UN or through international consultations as stipulated in the Sarkozy plan, or bring any degree of international understanding to the problem. This is, of course, now the major issue that we will be dealing with for years to come.

I would also like to say a few words about the victims of this conflict. The number of casualties has been the subject of major disagreement and speculation, both during and after the conflict. Nevertheless, it is clear that levels of population displacement have been very significant. According to a recent report from the Council of Europe, at the height of the crisis, around 150,000 people were displaced. In South Ossetia, a majority of the population, over 30,000 people, fled to Russia and North Ossetia. On the Georgian side, more than 120,000 Georgians were displaced at the height of the conflict. Currently, around 6,000 South Ossetians are still refugees in North Ossetia and around 80,000 Georgians remain displaced, of whom 20,000 or more will probably not be able to return to their homes for the foreseeable future. This is a major humanitarian issue that needs to be urgently addressed by the international community.

Could the conflict have been prevented? As I said earlier, in my view, this conflict was predictable. For months and weeks before the conflict we witnessed growing instability on the ground, frequent exchanges of fire, evacuation of civilian populations on both sides and a concentration of weapons in and around the conflict zone. We also saw a major failure of the international community to act in a decisive manner to prevent conflict. To illustrate this point, almost a year before the war began, there was a discussion in the European Union about the possibility of sending liaison police to the conflict zones, and the EU special representative to the region made a proposal for the deployment of a significant number of EU liaison police officers to these zones. It was eventually agreed that one person should be deployed in Abkhazia and one in South Ossetia. This shows the extent of the willingness of the EU to act at a time when the conflict was escalating.

I would like to look also at the role of the Organisation for Security and Cooperation in Europe (OSCE). The OSCE has been inhibited in its actions for many months and years, in part by a lack of consensus among its members and by a lack of resources. Russia blocked repeated demands to expand the OSCE military observer mission in South Ossetia. As a result, the presence of OSCE observers on the ground failed to result in early warning and early action in response to what was clearly a build-up to conflict. If a high-level meeting – of the OSCE Permanent Council, or an emergency ministerial meeting, for example – had been called in the weeks or even days before the conflict, or if the issue of the escalation of the conflict had been made public and communicated to international media, I believe the violence could have been prevented. Finally, the UN. I am surprised that the UN Security Council has so far failed to reach agreement on any of the issues relating to this conflict. I think that this failure calls into question the ability of the UN, and the Security Council in particular, to act in a situation in which its members have opposed interests in a conflict. A way needs to be found to engage the UN at the early stages to either prevent or contain conflict.

What are the wider issues involved in this war, and what are its implications for these issues? I believe that not only had these conflicts been ignored for a very long time, but support for the independence of Kosovo and NATO enlargement contributed greatly to the current crisis. The unilateral declaration of the independence of Kosovo and its subsequent recognition by many Western states should not be seen as a precedent for the Abkhazia and South Ossetia recognitions, but there is no doubt in my mind that these events galvanised the populations of the latter regions to seek independence in a more decisive fashion; at the same time, it was very difficult to explain to them why, if Kosovo could be recognised, Abkhazia and South Ossetia could not. I believe that this contributed to the deterioration of what was already a deadlocked peace process.

NATO enlargement and the Bucharest Summit also contributed significantly, by creating an atmosphere of insecurity around Georgia. The push for a Membership Action Plan for Georgia and Ukraine that was made at the Bucharest Summit in the absence of a consensus within NATO was counterproductive. Moreover, the adoption by the Alliance at Bucharest of the pledge that Georgia and Ukraine would become members of NATO without agreeing on criteria for their membership certainly created an atmosphere in which Russia felt threatened, and I believe that it contributed to Russia's decision to use force in South Ossetia when the conflict escalated.

So where do we go from here? There are several important issues to address. The first issue, with which the international community is currently very actively engaged, is the need to achieve in the shortest possible time the withdrawal of Russian troops from the so-called security and buffer zones around South Ossetia and Abkhazia. Deployment of EU monitors to the region is also urgent; I think it is very important that the EU is involved on the ground and that it assumes a greater role in promoting stability, security and conflict resolution in the South Caucasus. The next issue that we need to address is more broadly how to approach the issue of Abkhazia and South Ossetia. It seems to me that Russia's decision on recognition is irreversible, and I believe that it is important that neither Abkhazia nor South Ossetia – particularly not Abkhazia – is put in a position where it is pushed even further towards integration with Russia. We need to find a way to recognise the legitimate concerns of the populations of Abkhazia and South Ossetia and at the same time return to the conflict-resolution process. Recognition does not equate with conflict resolution. What Russia's recognition has done is to freeze the conflicts once again, with a new status quo that is further from addressing the root causes of conflicts and from promoting reconciliation and confidence-building between populations and elites in Georgia and Abkhazia and Georgia and South Ossetia.

We also need to think about how to develop the relationship with Russia in a situation in which, it seems to me, there are no clear mechanisms for engagement on this or other issues. We must return to the negotiating table to address the fallout from the August conflict and discuss future conflict-resolution strategies with Russia, not without it. In the meantime, it is extremely important that the humanitarian problems, particularly those within 'Georgia proper', are addressed quickly and decisively, and the donors' meeting to arrange funds for Georgia and the conflict regions will be very important in this regard. In the longer term, we need to think about what to do about NATO enlargement and about how to reassure Ukraine in particular. In my view, in the current environment, it would be extremely counterproductive to think about taking further steps towards Georgian and Ukrainian membership in NATO. We need to find other ways to reassure those countries that the international community will support them and help them to integrate more closely with the West. Decisions on NATO enlargement at this time will only escalate the conflict, not solve it.

My final point is that this conflict has no winners. It has undermined Russia's international reputation, weakened Georgia's chances of integrating Abkhazia and South Ossetia, and highlighted once again the weaknesses within the international system. The challenge now is to find ways to deal with this crisis decisively, but also to move beyond it, to find ways to once again begin addressing other important international issues in a cooperative manner. The South Caucasus will remain a pivotal region where relations between Russia and the West will be tested and where no security challenges can be addressed without their cooperation.

II: Perspectives on Asian Security

Keynote Address to the 7th IISS Asia Security Summit,
the Shangri-La Dialogue, Singapore, 30 May 2008

Lee Hsien Loong
Prime Minister of Singapore

Since our last meeting, we have had an eventful year of turbulence and rising global challenges. The Middle East remains a source of tension and instability affecting the whole world. Iran is pressing on with its nuclear programme against the objections of the international community. This is shifting the balance of power in the region, and increasing the risk of proliferation and conflict. The Israeli–Palestinian peace process remains deadlocked, with little prospect of progress. In Iraq, the troop 'surge' has improved security, although a more enduring resolution of the conflict between contending Iraqi factions remains elusive. In Afghanistan, the security outlook has been marred by continuing violence. Efforts to support nation-building and to stabilise the whole region will continue to test the political will of the peoples of the US and the NATO countries.

In Asia, too, there have been significant security developments, but the overall strategic environment remains benign. Regarding North Korea, the Six-Party Talks to contain the nuclear situation have achieved some results. Realistically, progress on this issue will be slow, because Pyongyang believes that its nuclear-deterrent capability ensures its continued existence, and is the only way that the world, particularly the US, will take it seriously. However, even if definitive solutions are hard to come by in the short term, the situation is manageable.

Within the region, relations between the key powers – China, Japan and India – remain stable and constructive. China is playing an increasingly crucial role in both regional and global affairs. It has made progress with its political renewal. At the 17th Communist Party Congress last October, a new leadership team was elected, which included potential successors. However, there has been no change in China's economic policies, which remain pro-reform and pro-growth. At the same time, China is putting more emphasis on sustainable development, environmental concerns and social equity. On the diplomatic front, China has stepped up its engagement with the UN Security Council and its participation in peacekeeping operations. It has contingents all over the world: in Timor Leste, Kosovo, Darfur and elsewhere.

China's relations with Japan are warming up. Prime Minister Yasuo Fukuda of Japan is continuing with former Prime Minister Shinzo Abe's policy of engaging and cooperating with China. Following last year's exchange of visits – Fukuda went to China and China's Premier Wen Jiabao went to Japan – Chinese President Hu Jintao made a 'warm spring' state visit to Tokyo this year. It was the first such visit by a General Secretary of the Chinese Communist Party since Jiang Zemin's acrimonious journey a decade ago in 1998. Both sides want to move forward and build constructive relations, despite unreconciled views of history and unresolved bilateral issues. In Tokyo, Hu said that there should be no grudges between the two neighbours, and that history was a 'mirror to look forward to the future'. Fukuda responded that both countries must 'constantly deepen mutual understanding and mutual confidence'. This pragmatic approach bodes well for bilateral relations and, more broadly, for stability in East Asia.

Cross-straits relations between China and Taiwan are also set to improve, with the election of Ma Ying-jeou of the Kuomintang as president of Taiwan. Ma has taken a radically different approach from that of his predecessor, Chen Shui-bian of the Democratic Progressive Party. President Chen had distanced Taiwan from China, slowed investment and trade, and sought to create a distinct and separate political entity and cultural, linguistic and national identity. However, there has been a decisive shift in attitudes in Taiwan. Nearly 60% of the electorate voted for Ma because they realised that years of pushing the envelope on independence had seriously strained relations with the mainland, caused Taiwan to be left behind, and, furthermore, upset the United States. They now wish instead to maintain the status quo of 'no reunification, no independence and no conflict', develop constructive relations with China and foster a more prosperous economy. Hu Jintao recently held a high-profile meeting with Wu Poh-hsiung, the chairman of the Kuomintang in Beijing, in which he stated clearly that China was willing to work with the new leaders in Taiwan to resume dialogue and build trust in one another. On political matters, however, China will be cautious, carefully calibrating its moves. It will also closely monitor Ma's actions and the trend of 'Taiwanisation', still in evidence in spite of the change in government, to determine whether its primary purpose is to simply emphasise local customs and practices, or to create an identity separate and distinct from the common heritage of the 'peoples of Chinese descent'.

India's weight in regional affairs continues to grow. In maritime security, India's reach now extends from the Indian Ocean to the Strait of Malacca and beyond. On the economic front, India has a 'comprehensive economic cooperation agreement', effectively a free-trade agreement, with Singapore, and is negotiating free-trade agreements with the Association of Southeast Asian Nations (ASEAN) and other regional partners. India's 'soft power' is growing, with Bollywood movies and Indian fashion gaining popularity abroad – indeed, enjoying considerable followings in Singapore. Nearer home, India is keen to improve relations with its immediate neighbours, in particular with Pakistan, which is just emerging from a period of political turbulence. India and Pakistan have resumed their dialogue on the issue of Kashmir after a six-month break. Both countries recognise that resolving this long-standing dispute will take time, but also that it should not hold back cooperation in other areas in the meantime.

This generally benign political landscape has helped to foster a closer regional network of cooperation. Southeast Asian countries are progressing towards greater integration, with the signing of the ASEAN Charter in Singapore in November last year and the targeted creation of a Southeast Asian economic community by 2015. In the broader region, ASEAN+3, which includes China, Japan and Korea, has become an established forum for concrete cooperation, including on mechanisms for economic and financial surveillance. The East Asia Summit, which is comprised of ASEAN+3 plus India, Australia and New Zealand, is also developing substance, starting with areas such as energy security and a proposal to revive the ancient Nalanda University in India. The balance between these groupings is still evolving, but the regional-cooperation architecture is beginning to take shape.

In the coming year, I envisage the continuation of some of the issues we are confronting today, but, naturally, also new challenges and uncertainties. We in Asia are following the US presidential campaign closely, because the critical issues of war and peace, of prosperity and scarcity, all hinge on its outcome. Singapore has no vote in the US election, but we have our wish list. I hope that the next president will do the following: uphold America's commitment to globalisation, free trade and international rules;

pursue constructive relations with China and other major powers; actively cultivate America's vital and diverse interests in the Asia-Pacific, especially in Southeast Asia; remain steadfast in the fight against terrorism; and, therefore, take a long-term approach towards Iraq and Afghanistan. America's role is especially crucial in engaging a rising Asia and integrating it into the global system. The emerging powers in Asia should have greater stakes in the existing international order. International cooperation is also key to tackling non-traditional security threats such as food shortages and natural disasters, which are increasingly trans-border in character.

Let me now discuss three important issues for the future. The first imperative is to uphold an open, globalised system that promotes economic interdependence between countries. The greater the stakes in one another's success, the more incentive countries have to cooperate and uphold a stable world order which fosters growth and prosperity for all, and the higher the price of non-cooperation or conflict. However, globalisation also confronts countries with daunting challenges. Spreading the benefits of globalisation widely among populations is a considerable task. In many developed countries, income gaps are increasing. At the top, incomes are zooming out of sight, widening the distance between, as someone once described it to me, the 'haves' and the 'have-yachts'. In the middle, incomes are stagnating; at the bottom, conditions are in some cases getting worse. Job insecurity, immigration and economic restructuring all contribute to a pervasive sense of insecurity among workers, who feel helplessly caught up in the process of change, rather than being the beneficiaries of a bigger economic pie. Even those not personally affected or vulnerable feel uneasy that closer interdependence may mean becoming vulnerable to foreign powers that may not be benign: buying up your companies, supplying you with important natural resources, and making you more dependent on them than they are on you. Hence the anxiety and debate about sovereign wealth funds. All this is fuelling deep discontent with globalisation, and provoking nationalistic and protectionist sentiments around the world.

These issues confront countries everywhere. Governments therefore need to address the anxieties of workers, help more people to become winners, and so build a broad consensus that supports globalisation and prosperity and resists protectionism and xenophobia. If countries pursue 'beggar-thy-neighbour' policies or erect barriers against one another, not only will we all be economically worse off, but frictions and rivalry between countries and regions will become more difficult to contain.

The mood in the developed countries is defensive, partly because the emergence of Asia is shifting the balance of power. However, Asia's growth is not a zero-sum game. Over the next 25 years, Asia's growth will contribute to a doubling in size of the global economy, and open up a range of opportunities for many countries. It is in the vital interests of the status-quo powers of the developed world to accommodate a rising Asia and to engage the region constructively. For their part, Asian countries are becoming more and more interlinked with the rest of the world. As this process continues, these countries' stakes in the international system will grow and they will need to take greater responsibility in world affairs.

The most important player in Asia is China. The Olympic Games in August will be China's coming-out party to celebrate its progress, its transformation and its opening up to the world. If carried off well, it will boost China's confidence, and help it to continue liberalising and opening up. If handled badly, it will stir up deep and angry nationalist sentiments within China, and fuel fears and suspicions of China in other countries, with serious long-term consequences.

The disruptions to the Olympic-torch relay in Europe and the US last month illustrated how things can go wrong. Tibetan activist groups seized this opportunity to embarrass China and to press their case. They organised aggressive demonstrations and protests along the route to capture the attention of the media and secure propaganda success. In some places, pro-China groups organised counter-demonstrations to fly the Chinese flag and the groups clashed. Images of the clashes were beamed live around the world. In the West, the images influenced public opinion against China and the Games. In China and in Hong Kong, the same images sparked outrage and sharp nationalist reactions, especially among young Chinese, who flooded internet bulletin boards and chat rooms with virulently anti-foreign sentiments. Some more sober voices in China have criticised this as an overreaction, lamenting how easily parts of China's public debate could so suddenly appear to return to the name-calling and vilification that was the norm during the Cultural Revolution. Chinese national pride and the desire to mount a successful Olympics are sincere and passionately felt. They have deep historical roots in two centuries of weakness and humiliation, and in the awareness that now at last China is becoming strong again. The international community needs to understand the strength of these gut emotions in Chinese society and in the collective psyche. At the same time, the Chinese people need to develop a sense of their new place and power in the world, and to learn how to engage the West with measured confidence. This process will take time on both sides.

For now, the issue of the Olympic torch has been pushed off the head-lines, partly because the torch is now in China, but also because of the Sichuan earthquake. But managing the Olympics continues to pose a major challenge to China. More unexpected incidents could arise, even during the Games themselves. How China handles them, and how the world responds, will have a major impact on the strategic success of the Beijing Olympics. Beyond the Olympics, the broader question is whether narrow interest groups will succeed in defining the international agenda on China, or whether China and the West can rise above these vexing issues to pursue strategic opportunities together. This will strongly influence whether China's emergence unsettles the international order, or China succeeds in its path to peaceful integration with the rest of the world.

Besides a peaceful ordering of global power structures and institu-tions, countries must also work together to tackle common trans-border security challenges. One immediate issue of concern is food. People have long worried that food shortages will come about as a result of population growth outpacing food production. Human ingenuity has deferred this Malthusian scenario for more than 200 years, but it could still happen in the future. On the demand side, the world's population is steadily increas-ing. Furthermore, with Asia's rise, hundreds of millions of people are becoming more affluent – as one minister described it to me, 'They used to eat one meal a day. Now they eat two meals a day.' This makes an enor-mous difference to their poorer compatriots and to poor people in many other countries in the Third World. On the supply side, misconceived green policies to subsidise biofuels are encouraging farmers to grow corn for fuel instead of food, squeezing the supply of food. In the long term, climate change will lead to more extreme weather conditions and is likely to reduce the supply of fresh water and arable land.

Over the next year or so, food prices may moderate with better harvests. In the longer term, the trends towards tighter supplies and higher prices are likely to reassert themselves. This has serious security implications. The impact of a chronic food shortage will be particularly felt by the poor countries. The stresses from hunger and famine can easily result in social upheaval and civil strife, exacerbating conditions that lead to failed states. Between countries, competition for food supplies and the displacement of people across borders could deepen tensions and provoke conflict.

We are already experiencing a small foretaste of this today. The recent sharp rise in food prices, particularly rice prices, has led to riots and unrest in several developing countries. In vulnerable areas such as Darfur and Bangladesh, large numbers of people are moving across borders, often illegally, in search of food and water. The issue becomes part of the diplomatic game. As one country has said, 'I am being blackmailed by my neighbours. They say, "Sell me one million tonnes of grain at the friendship price or I will send you one million refugees."' Even without a food crisis, major movements of people can raise tensions and cause serious problems, as seen in South Africa in the recent xenophobic attacks on immigrants fleeing unstable regimes and desperate poverty in Lesotho, Zimbabwe and elsewhere. Many of these immigrants are now having to flee in the opposite direction because South Africans who feel threatened by their arrival have viciously attacked them. In the event of a global food crisis, similar problems will play out on a much larger scale across the globe.

To avert serious problems, we need a multilateral cooperative effort. Individual countries need to increase productivity and upgrade infrastructure in their farming sectors. International agencies such as the World Bank and the UN Food and Agriculture Organisation need to promote research and development in agro-technologies to develop higher-yielding and climate-resistant crop varieties using the full power of modern bioscience, and, inevitably, genetic-modification techniques. Through the Doha round of trade talks, countries must work together to keep agricultural trade free and fair. Only then will farmers everywhere receive the market signals and incentives needed for them to produce enough food to meet increased demand. If countries pursue greater self-sufficiency and try to keep food production and distribution within their own borders, they will cause greater international tensions, because prices will become more unstable, food importers will scramble to secure their own supplies and poor countries will suffer not only greater privation, but famine and starvation.

Another challenge requiring international cooperation is the provision of humanitarian assistance and disaster relief. Emergencies call for prompt and effective action. The overriding priority is to save lives, but the responses of governments also have broader implications for domestic politics and foreign policy, especially when international assistance is involved, and when military forces are required. In Asia, this issue has been brought to the fore by two major natural disasters within the last month.

The massive earthquake in Sichuan province has been China's worst such disaster in decades. The last time a major earthquake struck China, in the city of Tangshan in 1976, the Chinese government was slow to react. It played down the disaster and rebuffed offers of help from the outside world, reflecting the attitudes of Soviet-style societies during the Cold War. This time, the government responded with a relief effort unprecedented in speed and scale. Within hours, it had mobilised more than 100,000 troops, police and medical workers to the worst-hit areas. Premier Wen Jiabao himself flew immediately to the disaster area to direct operations and to comfort the injured. This was all shown on national television and worldwide. The state response was matched by a spontaneous outpouring of compassion and support from the Chinese people. They rushed to donate aid to the victims, and converged in large numbers on the quake zone, providing food, shelter and medical treatment in makeshift refugee camps. The crisis rallied the country together in a tremendous sense of national solidarity, pride and public spirit.

It is not only China's self-image that has changed; media coverage of the earthquake has also presented a different face of China to the world. Satellite TV and the Internet carried wrenching images of devastation and suffering, and dramatic footage of soldiers and rescue workers wading through mud and gore to help the victims, working side-by-side with international NGOs and foreign rescue teams. Japan was the first country to send rescue workers to China, and the first country from which China accepted such help. It was a gesture of goodwill on both sides that will not have gone unnoticed. Rescue teams from Russia, Korea, Singapore and other countries followed soon after. The entire rescue operation was an extraordinary feat.

This is a view of China the world has never had before: a sympathetic view of a country in transition, confronting enormous problems, but also mustering huge energies and unexpected capabilities, as well as displaying a shared humanity. The response to the Sichuan earthquake showed how much China has changed, and offered a glimpse of its future as a more open and self-confident nation. The political aftershocks from this defining moment in China's history will be felt long after the ground has ceased to tremble.

The other major natural disaster was Cyclone Nargis, which struck southern Myanmar ten days before the Sichuan earthquake. The devastation in the Irrawaddy Delta is almost on the same scale as the devastation in Aceh province in Indonesia after the Boxing Day tsunami of 2004. Then, Aceh was able to recover and rebuild itself through the massive foreign assistance of the US and many other countries, delivered mostly by their military forces using aircraft carriers, dock-landing ships, helicopters and troops on the ground. However, this involvement had political consequences. The foreign military assistance convinced the separatist movement in Aceh, GAM, as well as the population of Aceh, that the separatist movement would not achieve independence. No country would support them;

they could not go it alone; they had to negotiate with the central government for autonomy. They did this, and a civil war was settled. Aceh is now at peace, more or less.

Myanmar is one of the poorest countries in the world, with limited capabilities and resources, and millions living in extreme poverty. Yet after Cyclone Nargis, the Myanmar government was extremely reluctant to accept help from abroad. Until very recently, it declined to allow foreign aid personnel to operate at all in the disaster areas, and insisted on sending all relief supplies through its own channels. It continues to decline offers from many countries to deploy military equipment and personnel for relief operations.

From the humanitarian standpoint, every day lost means more avoidable casualties and more unconscionable human suffering. The frustration of the international community at Myanmar's refusal to let it act faster and do more is completely understandable. However, from the perspective of Myanmar's domestic politics, the actions of the government should come as no surprise. The military leaders surely know that foreign aid will save lives and help to rebuild the devastated areas, but they also fear the political consequences of opening up the disaster zone to international aid teams. This might show up their incapacity and undermine their credibility and legitimacy. They are also highly suspicious that humanitarian aid might serve as a camouflage for a 'regime change' agenda, especially as some countries have talked openly about invoking a 'responsibility to protect' and mounting relief operations without the host government's permission.

It is regrettable that the Myanmar government has responded in this way. Myanmar's partners in ASEAN have all been deeply concerned by the massive suffering of the cyclone's victims, which a more rapid international relief operation could have minimised. ASEAN has taken the initiative, working together with the UN, to strongly encourage the Myanmar authorities to be more open to accepting humanitarian aid and allowing in foreign rescue and medical teams. These efforts have achieved some results, and we hope that they will continue to bear fruit. More can still be done.

In any natural-disaster situation, we must acknowledge such realities as these, and work out effective ways to cooperate to save lives, doing the best that is possible under the circumstances. This is why it is important to have a continuous process of dialogue and engagement among countries to build confidence, mutual understanding and trust. Governments must learn to work together on humanitarian assistance and relief efforts, as they already do in other non-traditional security areas, such as maritime security and counter-terrorism. Within the region, we can make use of existing structures such as ASEAN and the ASEAN Regional Forum so that when disaster strikes, countries can respond swiftly and deliver relief supplies and aid to the affected people and areas as quickly as possible.

The challenges of our time are more complex and multifaceted than ever before: adjusting to the rise of China and India, integrating Asia into the global order and dealing with the increasing scale of trans-border threats, such as food shortages, natural disasters and climate change. All of this adds up to a full agenda for Asia and for the world. Amid these challenges lie great opportunities: to reshape international institutions and norms, and to reframe the regional architecture to collaborate more effectively and build more enduring partnerships.

In this global endeavour, America's leadership continues to be indispensable. Dynamic and vibrant as it is, Asia will continue to depend critically on its links with the US and other developed countries. At the same time, the rising Asian countries will have to do their part as responsible stakeholders, and shoulder their fair share of the burden in the international system. We must work together across continents and across countries to reach a consensus on the big issues, and to make our interdependence work for the benefit of all.

Address to the 7th IISS Asia Security Summit,
the Shangri-La Dialogue, Singapore, 31 May 2008

Challenges to Stability in the Asia-Pacific

Robert Gates

Secretary of Defense, United States

In the 12 months since I last joined you, I have visited many countries represented here, including Australia, China, India, Indonesia, the Republic of Korea and Japan. Tomorrow, I will travel to see old friends in the Kingdom of Thailand, a long-standing ally. To those who worry that Iraq and Afghanistan have distracted the United States from Asia and developments in this region, I would counter that we have never been more engaged with more countries. Indeed, this is my fourth major trip to Asia in my 18 months in this job, and my second in three months.

As we carry on our discussions I would like to pause for a moment to offer my condolences to the many who have suffered, who lost loved ones, and who face incredible difficulties as a result of the recent tragedies in Burma and China. Amid the pain and the suffering, it has been heartening to see so much international cooperation by so many in this room. Many governments are doing everything they can to help save lives and rebuild livelihoods.

Over the past three decades, an enormous swathe of Asia has changed almost beyond recognition. By any measure – financial, technological, industrial, trade, educational or cultural – Asia has become the centre of gravity in a rapidly globalising world. This is an Asia where hundreds of millions have risen from poverty to better and better living standards, many into relative affluence, as a result of cooperation, openness and mutual security. At the same time, this new Asia is understandably eager to redefine itself and to redefine its security relationships with the rest of the world.

Today, I want to discuss these relationships and to emphasise three points: first, the United States is a Pacific nation with an enduring role in Asia. We welcome Asia's rise. Our continued presence in this part of the world has been an essential element enabling this rise – opening doors and protecting and preserving common spaces on the high seas, in space and, more and more, in the cyber world. This presence has offered other nations the crucial element of choice and enabled their entry into a globalised international society. Second, I want to stress that we stand for openness and against exclusivity, and in favour of common use of common spaces in responsible ways that sustain and drive forward our mutual prosperity. Third, and finally, as someone who has served seven United States presidents, I want to convey to you with confidence that any future US administration's Asia security policy is going to be grounded in the fact that the United States remains a nation with strong and enduring interests in this region – interests that will endure no matter which political party next occupies the White House.

For the last 60 years, America has added consistent value to the Asian security equation. This remains a reality today, just as it has been in the past. The security of all Asian countries, whether large or small, is strongly and positively enhanced by a strong US presence. America plays many roles in Asia: as an ally, partner and friend; as a routine offshore presence; as a resident power; and as an agent of professionalism and capacity in service of a range of non-military needs, such as disaster response – a point emphasised by our readiness to help after the tragic cyclone in Burma and the earthquake in China. Our alliances are the foundation of our security presence, enabled and strengthened by our relationships with partners and friends.

In Northeast Asia, mature alliances bind us to Japan and the Republic of Korea. These alliances are being transformed to fit the realities of the twenty-first century. The Republic of Korea is assuming more responsibility for its own defence as the United States reduces its footprint. We are realigning and refocusing our forces in Japan while cooperating in new areas, such as missile defence. 'Down Under', the Australians remain our stalwart allies and partners.

Aside from these primary security anchors, we maintain other formal treaty alliances throughout the region, including with the Philippines and Thailand. Over the years, each of these states has altered its treaty focus with us; it is natural that they should do so. Yet vital security interaction continues with both countries, with each aware that this special American connection adds to, or even enables, its freedom of manoeuvre.

Our relations with partners and friends, and our engagement in Asia, are more and more the fabric that binds together what is becoming a web of relationships, including our growing ties with India and our increasing engagement with China. While different in form and scope, we value these ties with Asia's two most prominent rising powers.

A few moments ago I referred to the US as a 'resident power'. By this, I mean that there is sovereign American territory in the western Pacific, from the Aleutian Islands all the way down to Guam. I have just come from that island where, with vital help from our Japanese allies, we are adding to our military presence with new air, naval and marine assets prepared to respond quickly to new contingencies. Our Asian friends, whether or not they are formally allied to us, welcome our growing presence on Guam. As the island's new facilities take shape in coming years, they will be increasingly multilateral in orientation, with training opportunities and possible pre-positioning of assets.

In recent years, discussions about a 'new security architecture' in Asia have assumed more prominence. We certainly share an interest in institutionalising a variety of forums to deal with region-specific problems, and we intend to participate in their evolution. In the meantime, we will continue to depend on our time-tested Asian alliance architecture, a framework that embraces many overlapping security relationships and which is still evolving. Our security activities include training, military-professionalism education, transit arrangements, joint exercises and the sharing of strategic perceptions.

As I say, these security arrangements run the full gamut. Last year, we participated in a multilateral naval exercise hosted by India. At this year's *Cobra Gold* exercise, Thailand hosted forces from Indonesia, Singapore, Japan and the United States. Nine nations, including China, India and Pakistan, were welcomed as observers. The *Cobra Gold* exercise no longer resembles what it has been for much of the past quarter-century – a bilateral, mostly conventional set of military manoeuvres with Thailand. This year's exercise focused on peacekeeping and humanitarian assistance – activities that form a vital part of contemporary security arrangements, as recent events illustrate all too well.

As you will know, American ships and aircraft were diverted from their *Cobra Gold* operational duties to help provide rapid relief to victims of Cyclone Nargis in Burma, pending country approval. Our ships and aircraft awaited country approval so that they could act promptly to save thousands of lives – approval of the kind that was immediately granted by Indonesia after the 2004 tsunami and by Bangladesh after a fierce cyclone last November. We worked with both these nations to alleviate suffering, while fastidiously respecting their sovereignty.

With Burma, the situation has been very different – at a cost of tens of thousands of lives. Many countries besides the United States have also felt hindered in their efforts. Despite the obstructions, we continue to get help into Burma and remain poised to provide more. We have shown in recent weeks our determination to give our entire support to saving lives, using every channel to get relief to the victims. We welcome the leadership of the Association of Southeast Asian Nations (ASEAN), and look forward to the quick emergence of a mechanism that can help international assistance reach those who need it.

As demonstrated recently, even with its ongoing operations in Afghanistan and Iraq, the United States military remains engaged with most Asian governments, doing more things in more constructive ways than at any time in our history. Regarding China, for example, I recently inaugurated our direct Defense Telephone Link with a call with Defence Minister Liang Guanglie. We have also begun a series of dialogues on strategic issues to help us understand one another better and to avoid possible misunderstanding. With India, we have, over time, deepened defence and security interactions with successive governments in New Delhi. There are many other examples of our defence cooperation, including with many of our friends in the South Pacific.

We welcome these security exchanges, some of which are modest, others quite substantial. Some countries have formalised their activities with us; others prefer a low-profile engagement. We favour any method that enhances mutual security and confidence. What we have seen in Asia in recent years marks a shift that reflects new thinking in overall US defence strategy. We are building partner-nation capacity so that friends can better defend themselves. While preserving all of our conventional military-deterrence abilities as traditionally understood, we have become more attentive to both 'hard' and 'soft' elements of national power, where military, diplomatic, economic, cultural and humanitarian elements fold into one another to ensure better long-term security, based on our own capabilities and those of our partners.

This approach brings various parts of the United States government together to work with diverse partners and friends across a range of shared interests – from old allies such as Australia, to those, such as India, from whom we were once too distant, to former adversaries such as Vietnam. In all instances, our involvement enables our friends in Asia to have more choice with their security-policy decisions.

In short, American engagement in Asia remains a top priority for us. Our alliances and partnerships are stronger and our relationships are always maturing and evolving to reflect changing times. Far from frozen in a Cold War paradigm, our presence in Asia is designed to meet our mutual challenges in the twenty-first century.

Which brings me to my second discussion point: whether we wish to persevere with attaining an open, transparent and mutually beneficial future, or whether we risk blundering into a future where competition and exclusion set the pattern. The foundation of prosperity in this part of the world – a prosperity that is fuelling the defence capacity of Asia's emergent powers – is respect for international norms and a common responsibility to protect common resources, even while pursuing individual agendas. Indeed, Asia's most determined advocates of sovereign prerogative have benefited the most from adherence to common norms. In my Asian travels, I hear my hosts worry about the security implications of a rising demand for resources, and about coercive diplomacy and other pressures that can lead to disruptive competition. We should not forget that globalisation has permitted our shared increase in wealth over recent decades; this achievement rests above all on openness: openness of trade, openness of ideas and the openness of what I would call the 'common areas', whether in the maritime, space or cyber domains. Even the 'open regionalism' espoused by ASEAN is part of this system – a rules-based system that has given states and their citizens unparalleled opportunity and prosperity. Without this system and without its rules, tensions can rise quickly when sovereign states compete over resources.

American policy continues to support efforts that maintain this system. For example, back in the mid 1990s, we welcomed moves toward a 'code of conduct' among states with competing territorial and resource claims in the South China Sea. We stressed then, as we do today, that we do not favour one claim, or one claimant country, over another. We urged then, as we do today, the maintenance of a calm and non-assertive environment in which contending claims may be discussed and, if possible, resolved. All of us in Asia must ensure that our actions are not seen as pressure tactics, even when they coexist beside outward displays of cooperation.

As we have seen in recent decades, the trust engendered by openness and transparency benefits every member of the region. This is the primary reason that the United States seeks more openness in military modernisation in Asia. Transparency enhances confidence and reduces competitive arms spending. The same transparency principle applies to the way in which sovereign governments make their national-security decisions. To give an example, in February this year, when confronted with a defunct satellite that was de-orbiting rapidly and posing the risk that it might spread toxic hydrazine upon re-entry, the United States organised an effective response in an open manner, making public the plan to engage the satellite well in advance of the intercept date.

As security officials, we here today know better than most how perceptions often drive reality, and how a lack of clarity about a neighbour's strategic intentions all too often prompts reliance, sometimes over-reliance, on counter-strategies and hedging that can, over time, yield to outright suspicion. This is a direction we seek to avoid. Instead, we desire to work with every country in Asia to deepen our understanding of their military and defence finances, and to do so on a reciprocal basis, in a sincere and open effort to avoid misreading intentions and so that we can continue our work as strategic partners.

For the most part, I believe that the overall trends in Asia are positive and where they are not, I see us working together more and more to address common problems, through mechanisms like the Six-Party Talks. I can assure you that the United States – because of our interests and because of our values – will not only remain engaged, but will become even more so in the decades ahead. And so the third and final subject that I want to discuss is the type of defence and security policies that the new United States administration is likely to pursue after it takes office next January. While I cannot predict the specifics of a new president's Asia policy, certain elements may already be discerned beyond the time-tested principles of strategic access, freedom of commerce and navigation, and freedom from domination by any hegemonic force or coalition.

Let me deal with the easiest proposition first. Any speculation in the region about the United States losing interest in Asia strikes me as either preposterous, or disingenuous, or both. America's status in Asia rests on long-standing interests and deeply held notions about the basic character of the United States. Projecting outward from our Pacific coastline, the US has had a cultural, economic, educational, geographic and political presence in Asia since the nineteenth century. However, we understand that our friends, partners and allies at times need reassurance. We will offer that consistently, and I hope I have done so today.

The next US administration seems certain to continue the overlapping, long-standing security partnerships that I have outlined. It will also inherit an agenda of worrying issues. This means no change in our drive to temper North Korea's ambitions, a policy not possible without China's valued cooperation. Beyond this centre-stage issue, I suspect that the new administration will also find strategic inspiration in America's dual role as a resident power and the 'straddle power' across the Asia-Pacific. Let me close with a few general comments. We here at this Dialogue all wish for a peaceful and prosperous twenty-first century, but we also know that nothing is guaranteed. The United States notes the stirrings of a new regionalism, a pan-Asian desire for new frameworks to encompass and thereby moderate inter-state competition. We welcome the resulting search for a 'new security architecture', a search that goes on in the context of a peace and order that prevail with the help and support of so many of our friends. This search will continue – after all, one can hardly suggest that it is appropriate for Europe, the Middle East and Africa to develop regional security institutions, but not for Asia to do so.

However, we do have some benchmarks. Firstly, we should avoid an approach that treats the quest for a new security architecture as some kind of zero-sum game. The fact is that the region as a whole has benefited in recent decades from cooperation on issues of common concern. The collaborative reality of Asia's security today is to the exclusion of no single country. It is instead a continuously developing enterprise undertaken with allies, friends and partners. It can only succeed if we treat the region as a single entity – there is little room for a separate East Asian order. Our second benchmark is a willingness to work with partners and friends to facilitate the evolution of security arrangements suitable to our common needs. We will work to ensure that the United States continues to be welcomed in this part of the world in the coming years, as it has been in the past.

It is for the next US administration to work with Asian leaders to identify these trends and to make them work for the benefit of all of Asia, a region to which the United States belongs and in which it shall stay. As the next administration calibrates and refines these important relationships, it is bound to be guided by a single imperative: to make each of our links more relevant, more resilient, more responsive and more enduring. For all our friends and partners in this part of the world, this remains our goal.

Special Address to the IISS–AIPS Korea Forum, Seoul, 26 September 2008

Charting a New Frontier: 'Global Korea' in the Twenty-First Century

Han Seung-soo
Prime Minister of the Republic of Korea

In celebrating the 50-year journey of the IISS and the inauguration of the Asan Institute for Policy Studies (AIPS), I am reminded of Korea's own historic odyssey. This year, the Republic of Korea celebrated two major events: the 60th anniversary of the founding of the republic and the inauguration of the Lee Myung Bak administration. Consider for a moment how much has transpired over the past 60 years. Imagine if we were transported back to 1958, the year the IISS was founded. Korea was shell-shocked and devastated by a brutal war. Endemic poverty permeated all levels of society and Korea had no modern industry, with just a handful of friends in the international community. Had any one of us predicted back then Korea's place in the world in the early twenty-first century, they would have been laughed out of the room.

Today, Korea is the world's 13th-largest economy, the world's third-largest producer of intellectual patents, and a global provider of cutting-edge IT products and services. Its shipbuilding, automobile, steel products, petrochemical, refinery and electronics industries, to name just a few, are world-class. The FTSE Global Equity Index recently upgraded Korea to advanced economy status. In addition to this, at the centre of international politics and global development, a Korean, Mr Ban Ki-moon, is playing a vital role as the eighth secretary-general of the United Nations.

Asia's rise and co-managing Asian transitions
The theme of this conference is 'Korea in the Emerging Asian Power Balance'. For the Republic of Korea, as the last Cold War frontier, this

subject goes well beyond academic discourse. How we craft Korea's national strategy and corresponding forays into the international system cannot but have critical ramifications for the Korean Peninsula and East Asia and, indeed, for global stability and prosperity.

Consonant with Asia's rise as one of the world's three core pillars, the regional strategic balance is being tested as never before. For the first time in modern history, three of Asia's major powers – China, Japan and India – are simultaneously sharing the stage. This has created new opportunities, but also challenges, for the world at large, and especially for Asia's strategically important states. Japan, China, India, the Association of Southeast Asian Nations (ASEAN) and Korea together account for over 40% of the world's GDP. The Chinese and Indian markets, even with ongoing fluctuations in the global financial system, continue to attract foreign direct investment and buyers across the world. Leading Asian products, intensifying entrepreneurship, and the accelerated globalisation of Asia's most educated generation are changing the face of Asian and, in many respects, global commerce.

Fortuitously for the world and for Asia, the struggle for dominance which symbolised much of Asia's turbulent journey over the last century has been largely replaced with growing intra-regional trade and an incipient East Asian community. While not nearly as advanced as Europe's, Asia's growing multilateral institutions and cooperative regimes, such as the ASEAN Regional Forum, ASEAN+3, the Asia-Pacific Economic Cooperation forum, the Asia–Europe Meeting and the East Asian Summit, all attest to the building of new norms, principles and practices in Asia.

Yet this same region is home to many of the world's most brittle traditional and non-traditional security threats. Clearly, guns in Asia have been silent since the conclusion of the Vietnam War in 1975. And, despite major-power competition, prospects for direct inter-state war in Asia or, for that matter, in other regions, have never been as low as they are today. But East Asia is arguably the new fulcrum of global strategic competition. Three of the world's five declared nuclear powers have direct strategic interests and presences in Northeast Asia. The world's newest nuclear proliferator, North Korea, continues to test strategic stability on the Korean Peninsula and in Northeast Asia. Five of the world's largest standing armies reside in Asia. Many regional actors are investing in new power-projection capabilities. While this trend is not synonymous with a classic arms race, ensuring the prevention of new security dilemmas in East Asia is the *sine qua non* of regional security in the early phases of our new century. On other issues, some scholars argue that democracy is today at bay in Asia, citing increasing democracy deficits, differing shades of authoritarianism and the gross abuse of human rights and human dignity in selected countries, and the rise of ultra-nationalism.

Thus, notwithstanding Asia's unparalleled economic progress over the past three decades, the growth in democratisation and the rule of law, and the rise to the fore of vibrant civil societies, the co-management of politics, security and the economy in a bifurcated Asia demands bold new approaches. Crucially important is the fact that if the world can no longer divorce itself from Asia, neither can Asia afford to extract itself from the world. The two are intertwined, irreversibly so, by forces and interests that intersect, converge, multiply and diversify at all levels of the international system.

Because of this, if we continue to cling to the status quo, I believe that Asia's 'economic miracle' will not be sustained. Korea and major East Asian powers are key stakeholders in an open world economy. We have benefited tremendously from this economy, and continue to do so. Yet the maintenance of a liberal trade regime and a healthy global economy, the prevention of cascading financial crises and the addressing of the problem of hunger in the poorest economies demands substantial input from all members of the international community. The responsibilities of the wealthier states, including members of the Organisation for Economic Cooperation and Development (OECD), are self-evident and will continue to increase in the years and decades to follow. But equally relevant are the tasks of preventing and mitigating the spillover of conflict from border disputes and ethnic tensions, controlling and rolling back nuclear proliferation and addressing a range of urgent human-security challenges that cannot be ignored or wished away.

This is what I mean when I say that Asia is joined at the hip with the rest of the world: we cannot afford to be bystanders. We can benefit from the international system if, and only if, we give back our fair share. Ensuring a more stable and predictable strategic balance in East Asia requires a 'new look', or paradigm shift, within and among nations. In a world marked by both unprecedented progress and equally pervasive threats and challenges, we must not be afraid of change. Indeed, when it is called for, we must lead by example. When necessary, we must make difficult, often wrenching, choices. And when circumstances demand it, we must have the courage to go beyond myopic national interests.

'Global Korea' and the Lee Myung-bak administration

The participants in this conference, individually and collectively, share two overriding missions: to generate new solutions for outstanding global, regional and national challenges and to play direct and indirect roles as critical agents of change. For governments, the tasks are equally crucial, if not more daunting.

President Lee Myung Bak assumed the presidency of the Republic of Korea in February this year at a historical turning point for Korea and Asia. For the most part, although Korea has continued to prosper over the past decade, it has also been evident that business as usual could not prevail. Many Koreans wanted change, such as a revitalisation of the Korean economy and the unleashing of new opportunities for clean growth and shared prosperity. They wanted to upgrade Korea's brand and its standing in the world community. Koreans also wanted a more responsible, mutually reinforcing inter-Korean relationship. President Lee answered these challenges and won the election with the widest margin since the restoration of democracy in 1987.

Over the course of the past six months, the government has put its major initiatives and blueprints on the table. As all of you are well aware, however, it has often been a bumpy ride. We have learned some invaluable lessons. But I am convinced that our democratic values, commitment to the rule of law and active engagement with citizens from all walks of life are unshakeable staples of a vibrant democratic society. We would not have it any other way – as British Prime Minister Winston Churchill reminded all of us, democracy is the worst form of government, except for all the others that have been tried.

Over the next four and a half years, this government will remain committed to a range of critical reforms and new approaches, including in the all-important foreign-policy arena and inter-Korean relations. Our overall goal is clear: ensuring the formation of a 'global Korea', a fully advanced, more responsible and more open nation that positively shapes Asia and the global village to the greatest extent possible within the confines of its national capabilities. In this context, I would like to share with you the cornerstones of the foreign policy of the Lee Myung Bak administration.

First, the restoration of confidence in and the outline of a new *raison d'être* for the critical Republic of Korea–US alliance. Over the past six months, three summit meetings have taken place between the leaders of our two nations. President Lee and President Bush agreed in April to forge a 'strategic alliance for the twenty-first century'. Bilateral ties have never been stronger, but much more work needs to be done. Active consultations are under way at all levels to expedite the ratification of the Korea–US Free Trade Agreement. The modernisation of key deterrence assets in parallel with adjustments to US Forces–Korea is proceeding on schedule. Moreover, the bilateral alliance stands ready to meet a range of contingencies on the Korean Peninsula.

Second, the expansion of Korea's 'Asia diplomacy' is a critical component of our government's regional initiative. Korea is an Asian power. Our destiny is inseparable from Asia's. We believe that Korea is uniquely positioned to serve as a role model for developing states throughout Asia. A traditional society with a deep sense of history, Korea is also one of Asia's most vibrant democracies. Korea's role is not to impose our developmental path on our neighbours and friends. This is neither desirable nor even feasible. But I believe that the 'miracle on the Han River'* demonstrates what a country can achieve with focused, clean leadership, the pooling of human resources and linkages with the outside world.

Our critical ties with our two major neighbours, China and Japan, need to be broadened and deepened. President Lee Myung Bak and Chinese President Hu Jintao agreed in August to upgrade Korea–China relations to a 'strategic cooperative partnership'. The economic relationship between Korea and China has surged forward since the normalisation of bilateral relations in 1992. Koreans have 'rediscovered' China after an absence of many decades. Likewise, an increasing number of Chinese students, corporate leaders and officials at all levels of government are interacting with their counterparts in Korea.

Since the beginning of his administration, President Lee has also emphasised the need for a new path in Korea–Japan relations. Our government is well aware of Japan's leadership role as the world's second-largest economy. We continue to cooperate closely on a range of common issues, including through the Six-Party Talks. Yet progress has met some stumbling blocks. Notwithstanding the need to strengthen this crucial bilateral relationship, our government also believes in the need for critical historical introspection. We are ready to move forward, but, as President Ronald Reagan always used to say, 'it takes two to tango'. A mature, future-oriented and historically aware Korean–Japanese partnership is a vital link towards a more stable and prosperous East Asia.

In this regard, we paid particular attention to the address made by new Japanese Prime Minister Taro Aso to the UN General Assembly a few days ago, in which he said that 'China and the Republic of Korea are each [an] important partner for Japan, and countries with which Japan must seek to

---

* The transformative economic growth experienced by South Korea (Seoul in particular) over the last 40 years of the twentieth century.

increase mutual benefits and shared interests. Japan must promote multi-layered cooperation with both of these countries.'

Third, we remain fully committed to the peaceful and diplomatic resolution of the North Korean nuclear crisis, through the Six-Party Talks and the exploration of new opportunities in South–North relations. Lately, however, North Korea's actions on a range of issues have been disappointing. The momentum towards nuclear disablement and dismantlement has been stalled by recent moves made by North Korea. Our government has crafted an inter-Korean policy based on mutual benefit and cooperation. We stand ready to provide a range of positive incentives to the North, including humanitarian and energy assistance, but progress in South–North relations should proceed in parallel with concrete progress in North Korea's denuclearisation. It is up to the North Korean leadership to decide the depth of the interaction they want to forge with the South.

In inter-Korean relations, patience is not only a virtue, but a necessity. We are mindful of the unique characteristics of South–North relations and the even more unique interplay of forces within North Korea. We look forward to building a more stable and mutually beneficial relationship. As North Korea works out a range of complicated issues at home and abroad, our commitment to the Six-Party Talks and to strengthening inter-Korean confidence-building measures remains unchanged.

Fourth, a 'global Korea' cannot be truly global without assuming its fair share of the common burden. Korea would not be where it is today were it not for the substantial flows of foreign aid, military assistance, trade incentives and educational opportunities that it received throughout its formative years. I have just returned from the United Nations, where I addressed the 63rd session of the General Assembly, reporting that since 2000, our overseas-development aid has tripled, with assistance to Africa increasing threefold in the last three years. We plan to triple overseas-development aid to $3 billion by 2015 and, to better coordinate our development-cooperation policy with the international community, we will join the OECD Development Assistance Committee in 2010. Korea has provided humanitarian assistance to countries facing food crises and will offer, in addition to its assistance to North Korea, $100 million over the next three years for emergency food aid and assistance in strengthening the agricultural capacities of developing nations. With first-hand knowledge and experience of agricultural development, Korea plans to assist in various areas, including farming infrastructure, technology and policymaking.

Our troops stood shoulder-to-shoulder with Coalition and host-nation forces in the reconstruction of Iraq and Afghanistan. As I speak, a

350-strong Korean contingent is helping to keep the peace in Lebanon as part of the United Nations Interim Force in Lebanon. In more ways than one, Korean security is no longer confined to defence and deterrence on the Korean Peninsula. We are reviewing efforts to more effectively combat the proliferation of weapons of mass destruction. As a cornerstone of the world's non-proliferation regime, the Nuclear Non-Proliferation Treaty must be strengthened. On the political front, Korean officials continue to provide election-monitoring advice to those who wish to study Korea's accelerated democratisation.

Standing at the midpoint between the creation of the Millennium Development Goals and the target year of 2015, we recognise that, in order to achieve what we pledged, we must redouble our commitment to these goals. But political commitment alone is not enough. We need solid economic growth and a coherent strategy to translate our commitment into reality.

While the rapid growth experiences of Korea have served as a useful reference for many developing countries, we need to move beyond the conventional economic-growth approach of 'grow fast, clean up later'. At a time when the climate change that is to have such a critical impact on the future of humanity is looming larger than ever as a global challenge, what we need is 'green growth'. In his recent address to the nation on the occasion of the 60th anniversary of the founding of the republic, President Lee embraced a vision of 'low-carbon, green growth' as a new paradigm for Korea's future development. We support the global vision of reducing greenhouse-gas emissions by 50% by 2050 and plan to announce next year our own voluntary mid-term mitigation goal, set for the year 2020. We are also launching an 'East Asia Climate Partnership', which will initiate $200m programmes over the next five years to support countries in East Asia in making their economic growth compatible with combating climate change.

The Korean government has just announced investment in 22 pilot 'new engine of growth' industries, including solar and other alternative-energy development, environmentally friendly cars, robotics, nanotechnology and biomedical sciences. Together with the private sector, we plan to invest nearly $100bn by 2013. The Korean government strongly believes that 'green growth' can serve as a new model for national development and international cooperation in the twenty-first century.

New horizons and new paths

East Asia's evolving power balance need not be marked by incessant struggles for dominance. We have shown the world the remarkable resilience, fortitude and development potential of East Asia over the past three to four decades. And, as Europe demonstrated through its post-war resurrection and the formation of the European Union, profound change can be achieved through cooperation. Just as no man is an island, so no country can prosper in isolation. Once branded the 'hermit kingdom', Korea knows the costs of prolonged disconnection from the outside world. In an era of pervasive globalisation and mega-networks, we are reminded constantly of both the possibilities and perils of accelerated connectivity. For Korea, and for the rest of East Asia, the key challenge lies in reaping the benefits of globalisation and openness while ensuring the safety and prosperity of those who do not reside in the so-called 'flat world' of the globalised economy.

As a young man, I could not have imagined Korea's remarkable transformation. From the backwaters of international commerce to leading global corporations, from seemingly predestined poverty to foreign-aid-donor status, from intensely nationalistic worldviews to multicultural prisms, the Korean odyssey is also Asia's odyssey.

But for all of our collective achievements, we stand on the threshold of challenges that defy easy solutions. Unbridled economic growth, intensifying energy competition and depletion of critical natural resources such as water, fish and forests are issues that we must jointly address. If the benefits of rapid industrialisation have been enormous, so have the costs.

Allow me to close my remarks by emphasising one critical point. Some commentators have spoken at length about the so-called failure of the West. It is wholly understandable that Asia and other regions should wish to attain greater representation in international organisations and associated institutions. But let us not forget the manifold contributions of the West. The West is, after all, the world's largest provider of foreign and humanitarian aid. It is a supporter and practitioner of democracy, universal values and human rights, including the rights of women and children.

Korea has shown that Western values and traditional values, religions and culture need not be mutually exclusive. They can coexist in a powerful synergy. This is perhaps one of Korea's greatest gifts to the world – its demonstration of a commitment to democratisation, globalisation and openness, even as it retains and honours Asian values. Korean democracy, like all democracies, is imperfect. Yet respect for human dignity, the guarantee of a liberal society and attention to diverse voices and opinions cannot be wished away or ignored in service of cultural or political exceptionalism.

As we embark on a new century, we are reminded of the indivisibility of global security and prosperity. All of us must contribute to realising the vital mission of more innovative security cooperation and policymaking in this context since, in this era of unparalleled challenges, failure is not an option.

Address to the 7th IISS Asia Security Summit,
the Shangri-La Dialogue, Singapore, 31 May 2008

The Future of East Asian Security

Lieutenant-General Ma Xiaotian

Deputy Chief of Staff of the People's Liberation Army,
People's Republic of China

Firstly, I would like to express my regrets over the huge loss of lives and property in the Wenchuan earthquake and the Myanmar cyclone. As a representative of a disaster-hit country, I would also like to express my appreciation to the international community for its condolences and the disaster-relief support it has offered to China. I would like too to thank the government of Singapore and the International Institute for Strategic Studies for giving me this opportunity to exchange ideas with you all on issues of common interest.

Today, we have a grand backdrop of the world's irreversible multi-polarisation, deepening economic globalisation and robust regional cooperation. China's future and destiny have grown closely associated with the future and destiny of the world. Facing a complex international and regional situation; intertwined past and current disputes; and traditional security threats combined with increasingly conspicuous non-traditional security threats, China has continued to hold high the banner of peace, development and cooperation and to unswervingly adhere to the path of peaceful development. This has been a strategic choice made by the Chinese government and the Chinese people in accordance with the trends of the era and the fundamental interests of the country. This is also our solemn pledge to the international community.

History tells us that if we wish to survive and create better lives in peace, we must rely on ourselves for sufficient defence capabilities. Strengthening our defence capability is fundamental to safeguarding national sovereignty and territorial integrity. China's land border is 22,800 kilometres long, the coastline of the mainland and the islands together is approximately 32,000 kilometres long, and China's maritime area covers 4.7 million square kilometres. We have a profound responsibility to maintain our territorial integrity and to protect our maritime interests.

There have been positive changes in the situation in Taiwan, which have led to a good momentum of development in cross-strait relations. However, at the same time, forces for an independent Taiwan will continue to agitate for separation. The notion of an independent Taiwan is still influential in Taiwanese society. The mission of opposing and curbing separatist movements remains tough.

Strengthening defence capabilities is crucial to effectively responding to multiple security threats, such as the international terrorism that has increased in the past few years, greatly undermining international and regional security. Terrorist activity, ethnic separatism and religious extremism within China's territory have intensified, seriously threatening the harmony and stability of society. And with increasing world economic integration and the soaring volume of annual import and export trade, the outlook on combating piracy and safeguarding sea lines of communication does not appear positive. We need to improve our capabilities for diversified military operations in accordance with these changes in security threats.

Strengthening our defence development is also necessary to keep pace with international trends in military development. Since the 1990s, many countries have accelerated their military development, mainly through informatisation. The renovation of military doctrines; research and development of high-tech weapons and equipment; and adjustment of military structures and staffing represent a revolutionary sea change in the world's military affairs. In the context of this revolutionary change, it is imperative that China's armed forces keep up with the momentum of international military development.

It is important to recognise that China's defence development and its economic growth are in harmony. Defence expenditure has consistently been within the limits of affordability. The nation's growing economy and fiscal revenue has given rise to logical demands for an increased defence budget in real terms; however, compared to increases in other sectors, the increase in the defence budget has been limited and moderate. In terms of how defence expenditure is apportioned, China spends two-thirds of its defence budget on expenses such as personnel costs, training etc. Compared with the advanced nations, China's defence expenditure is still at a low level, both as an absolute sum and as a proportion of GDP. China is a peace-loving country and the Chinese people are a peace-loving people. Despite the changes in the international situation, China will always adopt a defensive defence policy. We will not enter any arms race and we will not be a military threat to any country. We will never seek hegemony or expansion.

The Asia-Pacific is the most dynamic region in the world. The world's stability and growth is reliant on peace and prosperity in this region. The current security situation in the region is, on the whole, in good shape. Relative peace and tranquillity has been achieved, while diversity has also been preserved. The key is that all countries have been actively cultivating a security concept based on mutual respect and equality. They have been striving to build and develop equal, positive and stable state-to-state relations, and there are reasons to be optimistic. Peace, development and cooperation are the mainstream. Relations between key powers have been constantly improving. Friendly exchange between nations has been widening and deepening.

All this has given rise to extensive and multifaceted defence engagement and cooperation. Defence negotiation and security dialogues have promoted mutual understanding and strategic trust-building. Joint exercises and training have promoted practical exchange and cooperation among military forces, and increased their interoperable capabilities in response to new challenges and threats.

Regional hot spots have been cooling down, and the seeking out of common interests and a preference for resolving differences peacefully is widespread. The instabilities and uncertainties that cause regional tension have been declining. Owing to the joint efforts of all parties, the Six-Party Talks on the nuclear issue in North Korea are making positive progress. The regional security mechanisms of the Asia-Pacific are steadily progressing as the region forms tiered and comprehensive security-cooperation mechanisms. The Association of Southeast Asian Nations (ASEAN) Regional Forum, ASEAN plus China, Japan and South Korea (ASEAN+3), the Shanghai Cooperation Organisation and others are playing positive roles in maintaining regional peace and stability.

At the same time, we must be aware of the security challenges that the Asia-Pacific region still faces. Traditional territorial and maritime disputes are still not properly resolved. Ethnic and religious disputes have led to regional tension and confrontation, and the threat posed by such disputes and by separatism remains severe. The issues that have raised the most concern have been the expansion of military alliances, the development and expansion of missile-defence systems, space weaponisation and nuclear proliferation, all of which create instability regionally and even internationally, and upset the equilibrium and balance of regional power.

Peace is a product of parity, a balance of power and offensive and defensive strength. We urge the importance of the universal security of the international community. We oppose any action that sacrifices the peace of other countries to achieve the security of others, including the expansion of military alliances. The security interests and concerns of all countries must be respected and catered for. To build and deploy missile-defence systems and to participate in missile-defence partnerships in some areas in the world is detrimental to strategic balance, confidence-building and regional stability. Regarding the issue of space, outer space belongs to all mankind, and we should utilise it in a peaceful manner. We are opposed to outer-space weaponisation and outer-space arms racing. On proliferation, we must, within the framework of international law, proactively advance an international arms-control agenda and promote national security by using political and diplomatic means to solve the problem of the proliferation of weapons of mass destruction and their delivery.

We have seen a number of natural disasters over the past few years. Many, such as the Indian Ocean tsunami, the massive earthquake in South Asia and the cyclone in Myanmar, took place in the Asia-Pacific region, others, such as Hurricane Katrina in the US, elsewhere, but all caused grave loss of lives and assets. The armed forces of many countries have taken active roles in responding to China's own earthquake disaster and have actively participated in international relief operations. Their work has been significant to us. It has been shown that military forces have considerable capacity to handle non-traditional security threats. Exchange and cooperation between different military forces in this area is therefore necessary.

I would like briefly to talk about the participation of China's military forces in relief operations after this year's massive natural disasters in China. Between the middle of January and early February this year, the southern part of China experienced a disastrous and historically rare blizzard. China's military forces sent 667,000 men and made 89,500 vehicle journeys and 174 aircraft sorties to the region. They cleared a total of 32,000km of snow-topped roads, transported over 42,000 tons of relief materials, and evacuated and relocated 7.217m stranded victims. The military also took on the full burden of repairing the power grid, treating injured people and restoring public order.

When Wenchuan in Sichuan province was struck by a massive earthquake just over two weeks ago, the Chinese government exercised its philosophy of 'people come first' and gave top priority to saving lives. President Hu Jintao, Premier Wen Jiabao and other state and government leaders personally directed relief operations in the disaster zone. With a Class 1 national-disaster-response mechanism in place, military forces took immediate action in accordance with the Regulations on Military Participation in Disaster Relief and relevant response plans. They put in place a four-level disaster-relief chain of command and identified five specific areas of responsibility. More than 137,000 troops were sent to engage in full-scale relief operations.

By 28 May, we had dispatched 3,009 aircraft sorties and 110,000 sets of equipment, and deployed 207 medical, disease-control and psychological emergency-intervention teams. 3.248m sets of clothing, 1.086m first-aid kits and 41,694 tents were supplied. A total of 106,000 tons of relief materials was acquired and transported. Military forces monitored and cleared 41 dangerous 'quake lakes', pulled 27,000 people alive from the debris, treated 313,000 wounded people, relocated 660,000 stranded residents and tourists and repaired over 4,500km of roads. During the relief operations, officials and members of the Chinese government played a vital role in saving lives, comforting the public and restoring social order.

More than 30 countries and international organisations have responded to the Wenchuan earthquake, providing relief materials or sending professional rescue teams to China. Some of these countries have also offered the disaster-relief services of their military forces. On behalf of China's military forces, I would like to express our deepest appreciation for the friendly support provided by these governments and armed forces.

It takes joint efforts to curb common threats. In recent years, China's military forces have been actively contributing to the formulation of ASEAN Regional Forum guidelines on disaster relief. In addition to the ASEAN+3 Armed Forces Workshop on Disaster Relief, a further workshop on the issue will be held in June. By sending troops to join the Chinese International Rescue Team, China's military forces have also actively participated in international disaster-relief missions. The team has conducted search-and-rescue, medical-treatment and disease-control assignments as part of international rescue missions following the Indian Ocean tsunami, the Pakistan earthquake, the Indonesian Yogyakarta earthquake and other events. It has also assisted the Chinese government in providing humanitarian aid to 16 disaster-stricken countries.

China's military forces will, on the basis of mutual respect, mutual benefit and negotiation on an equal footing, step up exchanges between the militaries of Asia-Pacific countries. They will forge ahead with practical cooperation in counter-terrorism, peacekeeping, disaster relief, cross-border crime and other areas. We will cooperate with other countries to maintain regional peace and stability. We are committed to making assiduous efforts to build a harmonious Asia-Pacific region of lasting peace and shared prosperity.

Keynote Address to the 1st IISS–Citi India Global Forum, New Delhi,
19 April 2008

Shiv Shankar Menon
Foreign Secretary, India

I would like to speak to you today about India's opportunities and challenges. You might ask why. In the last two decades, India and most of the
world have gone through a period of unprecedented opportunities, which
have transformed both India and the world. It may be, however, that we
have arrived at the cusp of a shift in the balance between opportunities and
challenges, when challenges to the world system increase and the external
environment becomes harder for us all, including for India. In order to
examine whether this proposition is true, let us look at how India and the
world have changed, and at the opportunities and challenges that we face
today.

India transformed
In the 60 years since India's independence, a plural and diverse nation
has built and consolidated a democratic political order and has achieved
considerable success in its development tasks, both social and economic.
Economic growth, modernisation and the speed of technology-driven
change are transforming our society at an unprecedented pace. As a result
of 25 years of 6% average annual growth – growth which has owed much
in recent years to the reforms since 1991 – India is today in a position to
engage with the world in an unprecedented manner. Movements of goods,
services, capital and people connect us more closely than ever to once-
distant societies. India is more linked with the world economy than it
has been for centuries. Almost 50% of India's GDP is accounted for by

the external sector. Our needs from the world have changed, as have our capabilities.

However, daunting tasks remain. The two greatest challenges are to alleviate poverty and to achieve inclusive development by sustaining growth and bringing its benefits to all strata of Indian society. If we are to eradicate mass poverty by 2030, we need to keep growing our economy at a rate of 8–10% each year. The recent change in India's GDP mix has increased contributions from the industrial and service sectors; we need to ensure that our agricultural sector also achieves similar growth, particularly since a majority of our population still relies on agriculture. Our priorities include minimising developmental disparities across regions and peoples, reducing illiteracy and removing social barriers, maintaining a healthy balance between urban and rural development, and ensuring infrastructure development. At a minimum, this involves the efficient use of our resources, including human resources, enhancing education standards, improving productive skills and harnessing science and technology to our development. These are essential to sustaining and boosting rates of economic growth.

At another level, the maintenance of the current growth trajectory of India's industry will depend on the ability to meet our rising energy needs. For this, an effective energy strategy is necessary, combining augmentation with energy conservation. India's imports of crude oil and petroleum products are unlikely to decrease any time soon. Our dependence on oil imports requires proper management so as to lessen their inflationary impact and preserve a positive balance of payments, particularly given high global oil prices. Equally, if growth is to be inclusive and serve the goals of social justice, food security is essential for India. I will return to these themes later.

The world today

To successfully meet these challenges we also require an external environment that is conducive to India's transformation and continued development. This remains the primary objective of our foreign policy. We have a vital stake in the promotion of an environment of peace and stability in our region and in the world, which will facilitate India's accelerated socio-economic development, safeguard our national security, and lead to greater strategic autonomy. For the last two decades, conditions favourable to this quest have existed, generally speaking. And yet, when we look at the world around us, it seems less likely that this supportive environment will continue in the absence of concerted international effort.

Looking at the world from India, it often appears that we are witness to the erosion of the Westphalian state system and a redistribution of the global balance of power, leading to the rise of major new powers and forces. Our shorthand for this phenomenon is the rather inadequate term 'globalisation'. The twin processes of globalisation and increasing economic interdependence have resulted in a situation in which Cold War concepts like containment have very little relevance. The interdependence brought about by globalisation has put limits beyond which tensions among the major powers cannot escalate. What seems likely, and what is in fact happening, is that major powers will come together to form coalitions to deal with issues where they have a convergence of interests, despite differences in their broader approaches. In other words, what we see is the emergence of a global order marked by the preponderance of several major powers, with minimal likelihood of direct conflict amongst these powers. The result is a loosening of one-on-one relationships between powers in favour of each major power engaging with all the others, in a situation that might perhaps be described as 'general unalignment'.

The international situation has facilitated the rapid development of India's relationships with each of the major powers, and this has been apparent in developments over the last few years. India's relations with the United States have been transformed. They now span a wide spectrum of issues, including advanced technology, defence, space, agriculture, education, trade and other linkages. It is our hope that civil nuclear cooperation with the US and other friendly countries will become possible soon. Our strategic relations with Russia are rooted in a friendship that spans several generations and a relationship that straddles multiple areas of common interest. The trilateral India–Russia–China foreign ministers' dialogue continues to be productive. We are committed to strengthening our partnership with Japan. India shares a strategic partnership with the 27-member European Union, which is adding an increasing political role on the international stage to its considerable economic might. India is also engaged with the leading emerging economies of Brazil and South Africa, through the India–Brazil–South Africa Dialogue Forum.

Equally important have been two other necessary conditions which have given India space to work in. Due to India's rapid economic and social transformation, our engagement with the global economy is growing rapidly. India can do and consider things that we could not do or consider 20 years ago. This is reflected in how India perceives its own future, its ties with its neighbourhood and its approach to the larger international order. The second necessary condition, which obtains to a greater or lesser extent, is the peaceful periphery that we are attempting to build within which India's transformation can take place.

We will continue our efforts to develop close political and economic relations with all our neighbours. Our goal is a peaceful, stable and prosperous neighbourhood. India will remain a factor for stability and peace in the region. Our economic growth is having an impact in the region and there are increased opportunities for our neighbours to benefit by partnering India. We will continue to make unilateral gestures and extend economic concessions. The political challenge will be to set aside past mistrust and suspicions which have restricted the expression of our natural affinities, based on shared geography, history and culture.

The recent elections in Pakistan, Nepal and Bhutan have served to underscore the potential contribution of multi-party democratic frameworks to peace and stability. India will continue working with the new leaderships in these countries so as to enable each of us to pursue our shared objectives. It is our hope that the people of Bangladesh will also soon be able to choose their future and their leaders through free and fair elections restoring full democracy. Our destinies in the subcontinent are linked, and will remain so. One major objective is therefore the establishment of better connectivity in the subcontinent, both connectivity of the mind and physical connectivity. The resumption last week of rail links between India and Bangladesh after 43 years is testimony to this commitment. At the 14th South Asian Association for Regional Cooperation Summit in New Delhi last April, we set the goal of achieving, in a planned and phased manner, a South Asian Customs Union, a South Asian Economic Union and a South Asian Community. The popularity of such initiatives throughout the subcontinent indicates the strength of the impulse to remake these relationships.

This desire is equally strong even where difficulties persist. The unfortunate increase in violence in Sri Lanka reinforces our consistent position that there can be no military solution to the ethnic issue. It is necessary to find a negotiated political settlement within the framework of a united Sri Lanka, one that is acceptable to all sections of society. We will continue to assist Afghanistan in whatever manner we can in its reconstruction and in building a pluralistic and prosperous society. Equally, a peaceful, stable and prosperous Pakistan, at peace with itself, is in India's interest. We hope that Myanmar's ongoing national reconciliation and political-reform process will be successful. We recognise the need to expedite this process and make it more inclusive so as to ensure peaceful and stable democratisation. Our relations with our largest neighbour, China, are hinged on the mutual recognition that there is enough space and opportunity for both countries to grow and prosper.

With the Association of Southeast Asian Nations (ASEAN), India's engagement has been different. It is a civilisational engagement. India's 'Look East' policy is the central pillar of our relations and substantial steps have been taken towards integrating our economies, societies and institutions. The most visible achievement has been to meet the bilateral-trade target of US$30 billion a year ahead of schedule. Exports from ASEAN members continue to exceed expectations. An India–ASEAN fund has been established with an initial $1 million, and a proposal to establish a $5m India–ASEAN Green Fund is on the anvil. I am optimistic about the future of this partnership.

At the global level, India's engagement is geared towards playing a positive role in world affairs. It is this thought and aspiration that lies behind our desire to be a permanent member of the UN Security Council. A strengthened, more democratic UN is a basic necessity of the new global order.

Opportunities

As this brief survey shows, the last few decades have offered several significant opportunities for India's external relations. Can we expect this to continue? Certainly, India's capacity to utilise the opportunities that may emerge is today far greater than it has been before. As we seek to build a knowledge society, the revolution in technology, annihilating distance and enabling us to leapfrog stages of development, offers a significant opportunity. India's growing economy, linked to the world as it is, hopes to benefit from an open international trading regime, and requires an open rule-based international trading and investment environment.

Challenges

Paradoxically, it is these same interdependencies that pose the likely external challenges of the foreseeable future. Today we are told that the prospects for the world's largest economies, and for the world economy as a whole, are cloudy. As one of the beneficiaries of globalisation, India cannot be unaffected by a change in global economic prospects. India has a major interest in the success of the Doha development round, so long as it lives up to its name as a development round, and is true to its stated purpose of enabling an open, predictable, rule-based trading system. We will do what we can to make it a success, and to see that the concerns of countries, such as India, that have large numbers of subsistence farmers are taken on board.

Other recent developments that are worrying are the spurts in food and oil prices and the effect of these on energy security and food security. The world has yet to come to grips with these problems, and to deal with them on the basis of equity. The relationship between climate change and development is another such issue. India's commitment on this is clear and fair. Our per-capita greenhouse-gas emissions will not exceed those of the developed countries, even as we continue to seek to develop our economy.

Let us now look at energy and climate change in a little more detail, to understand why India adopts this approach. For India, clean, convenient and affordable energy is a critical necessity to improve the lives of our people. The average per-capita consumption of electricity each year in India is currently only 550 kilowatt hours, against a global average of 2,430kWh, a US average of 13,070kWh and a Chinese figure of 1,380kWh. At a projected growth rate of 8% a year to 2031 or 2032, the minimum rate needed to eradicate poverty, India needs to increase its primary energy supply by three to four times, and its electricity-generation capacity by five to six times. Even though we have been growing by over 8%, there has been an effective decoupling of our GDP growth from energy consumption, and we have not followed the energy-intensive growth pattern seen in the Organisation for Economic Cooperation and Development (OECD). Our present energy-generation inputs are predominantly thermal. We have abundant coal reserves that can be better utilised through cost-effective solutions and clean-coal technologies.

Linked to energy security is the challenge of dealing with climate change. The international community already has instruments for addressing this challenge, in the form of the painstakingly negotiated United Nations Framework Convention on Climate Change and the Kyoto Protocol. More than 50% of greenhouse-gas emissions are currently from OECD countries. India, with 17% of the world's population, accounts for only 4% of such emissions. And yet the adverse effects of global warming caused by accumulated and continued high emissions from industrial countries will largely be felt by developing countries. These unsustainable patterns of consumption and production must be tackled on an urgent basis. It is imperative that the developed countries in Annex 1 of the Kyoto Protocol urgently commit themselves to genuinely higher levels of greenhouse-gas reductions. The true freeloaders are those who have used up the world's carbon space for their own development and want to keep occupying it.

In discussing energy and food security, I do not mean to minimise the risks posed by traditional political complexities. In addition, there are fresh and major causes for worry – the changing nature of international security threats, such as terrorism and the proliferation of weapons of mass destruction, and the possible link between the two. India is ready to work with others to evolve a new international consensus to deal with these life-and-death issues. We believe that non-proliferation and disarmament are mutually reinforcing processes. The most effective non-proliferation measure would be a credible programme for global, verifiable and non-discriminatory nuclear disarmament, as reflected in the Action Plan presented by the late Prime Minister Rajiv Gandhi in 1988. In this, the 20th anniversary of the Action Plan, it would be fitting to renew joint efforts for general and complete disarmament, particularly nuclear disarmament.

In sum, the factors which threaten systemic stability come from large cross-cutting or transnational issues: food security, energy security, climate change and the environment, terrorism and the proliferation of weapons of mass destruction. As the world globalises, technology ensures that these threats also globalise. No single country can deal with these issues alone, and they require fair and equitable global solutions that involve us all.

Conclusion

All in all, it is probably too early to come to a definite conclusion that challenges now outweigh opportunities in the international arena. But the signs are that they will do so if we do not rapidly address clear and present elements of instability, and reform global governance and institutions to make it possible to do so equitably and efficiently, involving all those who can contribute to solutions. At the same time, in the near term, the continuing primacy of India's domestic developmental tasks and challenges is likely to mean that the fundamental tenets underlying India's global engagement, of benign and cooperative engagement, will continue.

Address to the IISS–JIIA Tokyo Conference, Tokyo, 3 June 2008

Asian Military Modernisation: Key Areas of Concern

Michael McDevitt

Director of the Center for Strategic Studies, Center for Naval Analyses

Military modernisation can take one of two basic forms. The first is simply replacing old systems or capabilities with similar but new systems, like replacing one's old Honda Accord with a new Honda Accord. More frequently in Asia, modernisation involves replacing old with new, while also adding entirely new systems or capabilities – the equivalent of replacing the family sedan with a newer model, while also buying a second car.

Trying to make sense of military modernisation and assess the impact of modernisation must start by making judgements about the operational characteristics of the system or capability. Is it an offensive, defensive, or multi-role system? Military modernisation goes on continuously throughout Asia, and not every modernisation activity is an area of concern, or presages an arms race. Quite the contrary, as adding systems or capabilities that are clearly defensive in nature and are carefully bounded in quantity and quality can actually contribute to stability. In an ideal world, if every country were able to defend itself from aggression from its neighbour, stability would be the result.

Arguably, what is taking place in Southeast Asia can be considered 'stability-inducing' modernisation, in that it improves defences without becoming a threat to neighbours. Much of the modernisation is oriented toward maritime capabilities, especially systems useful for the surveillance and policing of exclusive economic zones and the protection of commercial shipping. Maritime-patrol aircraft, air-defence enhancements – including fighters and small-frigate or patrol-craft-sized warships – land-based radar-surveillance sites and diesel submarines all fit within this category.

Similarly, in Northeast Asia, the Republic of Korea's ongoing introduction of a modest but capable blue-water navy does not threaten any of its larger neighbours. Like that of much of the rest of Asia, South Korea's economic health is increasingly dependent on trade, most of which travels by sea. As a result, Seoul has determined that it has a requirement to look after its maritime interests without needing to depend upon the US Seventh Fleet or upon its neighbours. This means that South Korean decision-makers, who are not experienced in things maritime and are embedded in what has been an army-dominated military culture, have been willing to make the not inconsiderable investment in building a modest blue-water navy. What this suggests about South Korea's long-term plans and concerns raises many interesting questions that are beyond the scope of this discussion. But the modernisation itself should not be considered an area of concern, because it is not destabilising.

Another category of modernisation relates to offensive weapons systems, or systems unambiguously intended for attack and not defence. This kind of modernisation is normally undertaken for one of two reasons: either to deter a neighbour or potential foe from attacking or harming one's interests, or to prepare for aggression against a neighbouring state.

In Asia, there are a number of instances in which the offensive purpose of a weapons system is not in doubt. Cyber-warfare is an emerging problem. In cases where it has actually been used, either by organised militaries or by state-sponsored hackers, it should be considered an offensive capability. Accurate conventionally tipped ballistic missiles and land-attack cruise missiles are clearly offensive systems, as are the airwings of attack aircraft carriers, significant amphibious-assault capabilities, long-range bombers and certain categories of land-based fighter aircraft. Today, China uses the threat of a massive missile attack to deter Taiwan from declaring *de jure* independence. North Korea uses missiles to deter attack by threatening US bases in Japan and throughout South Korea. The US posture in East Asia is largely offensive in nature, designed to be able to attack in retaliation and, as a result, to deter countries that may threaten US allies and friends.

There is only one obvious example of a capability being put in place to attack and seize another 'country', and that is the case of the continuing efforts on the part of China's People's Liberation Army (PLA) to develop the systems and capabilities necessary to capture Taiwan. Because China claims that Taiwan is a renegade province and that this an internal Chinese sovereignty issue, it naturally rejects the argument that modernisation aimed at a successful capture is offensive in nature. But the reality remains that capabilities useful for the Taiwan mission would also be useful in a campaign against any Taiwan-sized island.

On the Korean peninsula, it is less clear whether the forward-postured North Korean Army is in place so that it can attack the South, or whether it is in its current posture to defend against an attack from the South. At the June 2008 Shangri-La Dialogue, the new South Korean Minister of Defence explicitly offered the judgement that it was an offensive posture. This is a case in which transparency is lacking, and I suspect that Pyongyang prefers this ambiguity, since it is a powerful deterrent to any offensive action by the US against its nuclear-weapons programme.

The military modernisation associated with these two situations clearly falls into the category of 'area of concern', even though efforts to mitigate the negative impacts of these modernisations have been going on for some time. In the case of Korea, the South has made adequate defensive preparations, so much so that the US is confident enough in the Republic of Korea Army that it is not baulking at turning over responsibility for defence against an invasion: the US role will, over the next few years, transition to backstopping the Republic of Korea Army with US air and naval power.

In the case of Taiwan, the Chinese threat to use force has been a feature of the Asian security scene for more than 50 years. What is different today is that Beijing's threat is actually credible. It is credible in the sense that, though it is not yet able to capture the island, it can militarily 'punish' Taiwan by bombarding it with hundreds of missiles. In this situation, it is the combination of the willingness of the people of Taiwan to endure a bombardment, the efforts being made by the Taiwan authorities to harden key facilities against bombardment and the threat of US intervention in defence of Taiwan that has sustained stability. Obviously, it is the state of the cross-strait political relationship that will determine whether in the future Beijing would be willing to actually 'pull the trigger'. Today, for the first time this decade, the political situation could be characterised as hopeful.

While categorising systems and capabilities is relatively straightforward, more and more modern weapons systems are designed to be multi-role. In these cases, they can be used either to attack or to defend; they are not purely offensive or purely defensive. Multi-role aircraft are perhaps the best example. The aircraft's role is determined by the weapons it is fitted to carry, the avionics software package installed and the training the crew has received. In cases where the nature of potentially threatening weapons systems is unclear, officials charged with defence responsibilities have to look at a country's military capability in the context of its intentions. This is why issues of transparency are intimately linked with assessments of modernisation.

This brings me to another way in which modernisation can have an impact on stability. This is the circumstance created when a country fields defensive capabilities to assure its defences but in so doing puts the security of its near neighbours in jeopardy. Political scientists call this a 'security dilemma'. Arguably, this is what is going on today between China, the United States and China's Northeast Asian neighbours and US allies Japan, South Korea and Taiwan. This is an area of great concern.

Historical stability of alliance-based security architecture

For almost 50 years, Asia's security environment has been stable and relatively predictable. After the 1953 armistice that ended combat in Korea, Asia's security environment quickly settled into a unique balance of power, in which the continental powers of the Soviet Union and China were balanced by the US-led coalition of Asian littoral powers.

There are a number of reasons why stability persisted, but arguably the most important one is that a real military balance existed.* The military capability of each side was effectively limited to its domain – the continent, or the oceans. Each side was able to militarily 'trump' any attempt by the other to intrude in a militarily significant way on its domain. The USSR and China were safe from invasion thanks to their large armies, vast territories and nuclear weapons. US friends and allies were safe from invasion and maritime blockade thanks to US air and sea power, which was constantly in play because of alliance obligations.

Effects of modernising China on the continental–maritime strategic balance

Throughout China's long history, the country's strategic orientation could be categorised as continental, and hence its strategic tradition – its way of thinking about and framing strategic issues – has been largely focused on land war. Today, however, the risk of cross-border aggression is no longer a serious security concern for Beijing. The combination of adroit Chinese diplomacy within a contextual framework of globalisation, international

---

* During much of this period, China was preoccupied by the internal turmoil of the Great Leap Forward and the Cultural Revolution, and support for revolutionary movements in Southeast Asia. The Soviet Union was decidedly Eurocentric in its focus, and its out-of-area military operations centred on small-scale deployments to bases in Vietnam.

norms of behaviour that eschew cross-frontier aggression and the deterrent value of nuclear weapons has substantially diminished the likelihood of cross-border aggression. The threat of invasion, the primary worry of Chinese and indeed most Eurasian strategists for many centuries, has all but disappeared.

As globalisation proceeds, economic growth is increasingly dependent on trade, and most traded goods travel in containers loaded on ships. As a result, security on the high seas is a growing preoccupation for countries that historically were not strategically focused on the maritime domain. I have already mentioned South Korea; China is also in the midst of this evolving strategic zeitgeist. While its land frontiers are secure, Beijing faces a host of outstanding sovereignty claims and unresolved strategic issues that are maritime in nature. Specifically:

- Taiwan is an island. It is the combination of Taiwan's air defence and the threat of intervention by the US military (primarily the US Navy) that effectively keeps the Taiwan Strait a moat, rather than a highway open to the PLA.
- Perhaps as strategically significant as Taiwan to a PLA planner is the geostrategic reality that China's economic centre of gravity is its east coast, which, being a seaboard, is extremely vulnerable to attack from the sea – a military operation the United States is uniquely suited to executing.
- Territorial disputes with Japan over islands and seabed resources in the East China Sea remain unresolved and, as the price of oil continues to soar, the economic stakes become higher, representing a potential flashpoint where Sino-Japanese interests are contested (although the recent Sino-Japanese summit may lead to fair compromise).
- Unsettled territorial disputes, and concomitant resource issues, remain with respect to the Spratly Islands and the South China Sea.
- China's entire national strategy of reform and opening up depends largely upon maritime commerce. The Chinese economy is driven by the combination of exports and imports, which together account for almost 75% of the country's GDP. This trade travels mainly by sea.
- Finally, there is the issue of energy security or, as President Hu Jintao has characterised it, China's 'Malacca dilemma'. It has become commonplace to observe that China will increasingly depend upon

foreign sources of oil and natural gas, most of which come by sea
and must pass through the Indonesian straits to reach China.

In addition, Beijing's primary military competitor is the United States,
which is the world's foremost naval power and which maintains, as it has
for the past 50 years, a significant naval presence on China's doorstep.
Should China elect to use force to resolve either reunification with Taiwan
or outstanding maritime claims, the US is the one country that could militarily deny it success.

All of these factors, plus China's historical experience since the 1840s,
have generated a 'demand signal' that has caused China to field weapons
systems and capabilities that can protect its maritime approaches. China
is thus introducing an element of military competition into a maritime
region that has been the preserve of the United States and its allies for
the past half-century, and this is beginning to have the effect of upsetting
the five-decade-old balance of power between continental and maritime
powers that has been so successful in preserving stability in the region.

What is China doing?

Specifically, China is putting in place a credible method for denying
access to US forces by knitting together broad-area ocean-surveillance
systems, a large number of submarines, land-based aircraft with cruise
missiles, and ballistic-missile systems that can target ships on the high
seas. The operational objective is to keep US naval power as far away
from China as possible in the event of conflict. It closely resembles the
operational concept that the Soviet Union, another continental power
attempting to protect its maritime approaches, had in place by the end
of the Cold War.

According to the latest US Defense Department report to the US
Congress on military power, key elements of China's capability are still
in the testing stage. If, however, China succeeds in introducing a credible anti-ship ballistic missile and an associated surveillance and targeting
system, coupled with other proven conventional capabilities such as quiet,
conventionally powered submarines, it will have introduced a destabilising element into the regional military balance.

By working to achieve security on its maritime frontier, Beijing is
creating a dynamic that will, as China's own maritime-security situation
improves, make the security environment worse for Japan, Taiwan and
potentially South Korea, because a central element of its strategy is to keep
US power as far away from East Asia as possible.

US interests and obligations depend on sustained access to East Asia, and China's offshore strategy is increasingly aimed at denying that access. The United States has characterised China's approach as 'anti-access' because, if successfully executed, it could deny the US the ability to operate its naval and air forces freely along the littoral of East Asia. In effect, for sensible strategic reasons, China and the United States are pursuing two mutually contradictory approaches: access denial versus assured access. This is a serious issue.

Conclusion

This suggests that the military balance and concomitant modernisation of forces in East Asia will be in a constant state of evolution, as the US and its allies work to preserve existing advantages as the PLA develops new capabilities – all rising on the same tide, as it were. As a result, military-to-military engagement between the US military and the PLA, while necessary and appropriate, will tend to be coloured with elements of suspicion or concern, as each side participates in what could be termed 'capabilities competition'.

Even with the prospect of a much less tense cross-strait relationship, Beijing has not yet persuaded itself that it can afford to 'take its finger off the trigger' in relation to Taiwan. Until the threat of military force is removed from the table, each side will work to deter the other regarding the use of force over Taiwan. This will fuel the capabilities competition.

Beyond the direct issue of Taiwan, the competition is also a factor in whether the rest of the region views the US as a credible ally or a credible offshore balancer. Credibility is normally discussed in terms of Washington's political will to act; this stems from the assumption that the US has the *ability* to act if it so chooses. That assumption could change if the region comes to believe that Beijing's access-denial concept is a viable operational capability. This concern will continue to provide a strong incentive for Washington to give its Asia-Pacific modernisation efforts high priority.

Background Paper for IISS–JIIA Tokyo Conference, Tokyo, 2–4 June 2008

Asian Environmental Concerns

Jeffrey Mazo

Managing Editor, *Survival*, IISS

In its fourth *Global Environmental Outlook* report published last year, the United Nations Environment Programme (UNEP) identified transport and urban air quality, freshwater stress, valuable ecosystems, agricultural land use and waste management as the priority environmental issues for the Asia-Pacific region. These interrelated problems directly affect the sustainability of economic growth and development. At a ministerial conference on environment and development in Asia and the Pacific in Seoul in March 2005, ministers endorsed a policy of environmentally sustainable economic growth, or 'green growth', and in August another ministerial meeting in Jakarta reaffirmed a regional commitment to the UN Millennium Development Goals, including Goal 7, 'Ensure Environmental Sustainability'. Yet despite some movement, no country has made significant progress towards meeting this goal. Environmental problems continue to threaten regional development, and will be significantly exacerbated by global warming and climate change. Environmental problems are not limited to the developing countries of the region, although developed countries such as Japan and South Korea generally have better technical capability and more robust and better-enforced national legal and regulatory frameworks to cope with environmental concerns.

Underlying causes

As both absolute population numbers and per-capita economic output and consumption in Asia rise, so too do adverse environmental impacts

Region	Country	Population ('000s)		Percentage change
		2005	2050	
East Asia	China	1,321,959	1,418,350	1.07
	North Korea	23,616	24,666	1.04
	Japan	127,897	102,511	−0.80
	Mongolia	2,581	3,388	1.31
	South Korea	47,870	42,327	−0.88
	Regional total	**1,523,923**	**1,591,242**	**1.04**
South Asia	Bangladesh	153,281	254,084	1.66
	Bhutan	637	935	1.47
	India	1,134,403	1,658,270	1.46
	Myanmar	47,967	58,709	1.22
	Nepal	27,094	51,891	1.92
	Pakistan	158,081	292,205	1.85
	Sri Lanka	19,121	18,715	0.98
	Regional total	**1,540,584**	**2,334,809**	**1.52**
Southeast Asia	Brunei	374	681	1.82
	Cambodia	13,956	25,114	1.80
	Indonesia	226,063	296,885	1.31
	Laos	5,664	9,290	1.64
	Malaysia	25,653	39,631	1.54
	Philippines	84,566	140,466	1.66
	Singapore	4,327	5,026	1.16
	Thailand	63,003	67,376	1.07
	Timor Leste	1,067	3,462	3.24
	Vietnam	85,029	119,971	1.41
	Regional total	**509,702**	**707,902**	**1.39**
	Total	**3,574,209**	**4,633,953**	**1.30**

Source: Population Division of the Department of Economic and Social Affairs of the United Nations Secretariat, *World Population Prospects: The 2006 Revision* and *World Urbanization Prospects: The 2005 Revision*, http://esa.un.org/unpp.

and demands on resources. According to the Population Division of the United Nations, the population of East, South and Southeast Asia rose from 2.2 billion to 3.6bn between 1975 and 2005, and is projected to reach 4.6bn by 2050 (see table above). At the same time, the percentage of the Asian population living in cities has risen from 24% in 1975 to 37% in 2000, with 54% projected for 2030, as a concomitant of rapid and continuing economic growth, increasing prosperity and integration into the global economy. The standard of living and economic expectations of people in developing countries in the region, especially China, India and the states of Southeast Asia, continue to rise, with associated increases in the per-capita 'ecological footprint'. This growth lifted 270 million people out of poverty between 1990 and 2004, but nearly 670m are still living on less than a dollar a day and 500m are undernourished, the bulk of them in South and

Southeast Asia. As national and international development efforts succeed in improving their lot, there are questions as to whether this growth is sustainable. Some of these questions relate to availability of and competition for non-renewable resources such as oil, minerals and water. Others involve the direct and indirect health and security consequences of environmental pollution from more, and more intensive, industry, transport and agriculture.

Environmental threats
Water quality and scarcity
UNEP estimates that 655m Asians, or 17.6% of the population, lack access to safe water, due to a combination of absolute water availability and quality problems. As greater demand leads to increased reliance on non-renewable groundwater, some 200m people in the region may be affected by naturally occurring arsenic contamination, with another

Per capita ecological deficit/reserve, 2003 (global hectares)

Mongolia	8.7
Malaysia	1.5
Laos	0.4
Myanmar	0.4
Cambodia	0.1
Indonesia	0.0
Vietnam	−0.1
Bangladesh	−0.2
Nepal	−0.2
Pakistan	−0.3
India	−0.4
Thailand	−0.4
World	−0.5
Philippines	−0.5
Asia-Pacific	−0.6
Sri Lanka	−0.6
North Korea	−0.8
China	−0.9
South Korea	−3.5
Japan	−3.6

Figures represent the difference between the biocapacity (the capacity of the ecosystem to produce useful biological materials and to absorb waste materials generated by humans, using current management schemes and extraction) and the ecological footprint (a measure of how much biologically productive land and water an individual, population or activity requires to produce all the resources it consumes and to absorb the waste it generates using prevailing technology and resource-management practices), expressed in gha, a measure of area normalised to the area-weighted average productivity of biologically productive land and water. If there is a regional or national ecological deficit, it means that the region is either importing biocapacity through trade or liquidating regional ecological assets. Source: Global Footprint Network, http://www.footprintnetwork.org.

129m in India and China at risk from naturally occurring fluoride. At least 16 countries in the region, including China, India, Pakistan and the Philippines, have unsustainable rates of groundwater extraction. Industrial and organic pollution (including fertiliser run-off and sewage) and disposal of electronic equipment and hazardous waste, much of it illegally imported from developed countries, lead to biological and heavy-metal contamination of groundwater. Water shortages have also affected industrial development in China, India and Thailand; China estimates losses at $28bn per year in industrial output in recent years. Dams constructed for electricity generation, flood control and seasonal availability of water supplies alter ecosystems both upstream and downstream, and displace people from their homes. China's Three Gorges Dam alone, on which structural work was completed in 2006, has displaced nearly 1.5m people.

Land
Land degradation is a serious problem in many parts of Asia. Withdrawal of groundwater has caused salinisation of the soil and desertification, in turn leading to increased erosion. Contamination of soil from pesticides has increased due to the intensification and expansion of agriculture. Industrial pollution and waste disposal have further contributed to a decline in soil quality. Although rates of deforestation from commercial logging (some of it illegal), agricultural expansion and dam building are slowing, and in places forest is actually returning, on balance forest cover continues to decline, particularly in South and Southeast Asia. Deforestation has increased erosion rates and reduced water levels in rivers. The problem is particularly acute in marginal upland areas.

Air quality
Air-quality problems stem directly from human activity or indirectly from water scarcity and land degradation. The World Health Organisation estimates that air pollution contributes to more than 500,000 premature deaths in the Asia-Pacific region each year. The economic impact of air pollution in a typical megacity (a city with a population over 10m, of which there are 12 in the region) has been estimated at $100–300m per year. Increasing numbers of motor vehicles and the use of poor-quality fuels for heat and power generation have led to extremely high levels of particulates, lead, carbon monoxide and other pollutants. Sulphur and nitrogen-oxide emissions lead to acid rain, which has direct effects on human health and ecosystems, and leads to the acidification of soil and water supplies.

Key environmental issues for Asia

Region	Water	Land	Air	Marine	Natural Disasters
East Asia	• Industrial pollution • Heavy-metal contamination • Organic pollution	• Soil erosion and contamination • Desertification • Habitat destruction • Invasion of alien species	• Sand storms • Acidification • Vehicular and industrial emissions • Urban air pollution	• Overfishing • Destruction of coastal wetlands • Coastal eutrophication • Red tides • Heavy-metal contamination	• Flood • Drought
Southeast Asia	• Water contamination and water-borne diseases • Groundwater contamination • Industrial pollution • Watershed management • Organic pollution	• Forest fires • Deforestation in watershed areas • Logging • Shifting cultivation • Degradation of forest ecosystems • Soil erosion • Soil contamination • Decline of soil fertility	• Vehicular congestion and emissions • Particulate emissions • Seasonal smoke and haze • Transboundary pollution from forest fires	• Loss of coastal mangrove habitats • Overfishing • Coral-reef degradation • Oil spills • Tourist developments in coastal regions	• Flooding
South Asia	• Limited access to potable water • Water-borne diseases • Arsenic contamination of drinking water • Seasonal limitations in availability of natural freshwater resources • Depletion of aquifers • Organic pollution • Industrial pollution	• Soil erosion • Over-grazing • Desertification • Deforestation • Declining arable per capita • Food security • Habitat loss/degradation • Poaching	• Urban air pollution • Respiratory diseases • Indoor air pollution in rural areas	• Coastal habitat loss • Depletion of mangroves for aquaculture • Coral-reef degradation • Beach erosion	• Flood • Cyclone • Landslides • Drought

Source: United Nations Environment Programme, Regional Resources Centre for Asia and the Pacific. Does not take into account impact of climate change.

The impact of pollution from vehicles is significantly increased by traffic congestion in dense urban areas.

Springtime sand and dust storms (the so-called 'yellow dust'), aggravated by the spread of deserts in Xingjang and Mongolia due to groundwater depletion, salinisation and overgrazing, damage crops and machinery, cause respiratory problems and social and economic disruption, and spread toxic soil contaminants. Such storms occur every year with varying severity, and cause millions of dollars in economic damage, principally in China, North and South Korea and Japan.

Uncontrolled forest and peat fires from land clearance in Indonesia create a haze that causes health problems in Indonesia, Malaysia, Thailand, Brunei and Singapore for large parts of the year. The worst event was in 1997–98, when tens of thousands of people were hospitalised and economic damage was estimated at $9bn. International efforts to reduce the problem since then have had some effect, but the 2006 haze was the worst since 1997 and 2008 is expected to be even more severe. South Asia is affected by a similar 'brown cloud' from domestic and industrial pollution. The timing and severity of these clouds are affected by the timing of the monsoons and cyclical weather phenomena like El Niño and La Niña.

Coastal and maritime zones
Run-off of polluted water from rivers, erosion of contaminated soil and contamination of expanding port areas all damage coastal and maritime ecosystems. Cities such as Tokyo, Jakarta, Shanghai, Manila, Osaka, Tianjin and Bangkok all experienced major subsidence during the twentieth century due to groundwater withdrawal. Oil spillage from increasing tanker traffic and offshore oil drilling is also a growing problem, particularly in Chinese coastal waters. Fish catches in the region increased until about 2001, but have since declined due to overfishing and environmental damage; marine species in the eastern Indian Ocean are particularly vulnerable. In Southeast Asia, coastal mangrove forests are being destroyed to make way for intensive aquaculture, which, although producing significant protein resources, damages commercial fisheries and causes land degradation and water contamination. Expanding tourism and coastal development create similar problems. Coral reefs, which support fisheries, are at risk, especially in Southeast Asia.

Food security
Food yields and hence overall food production have kept pace with or even outstripped population growth in the last four decades, but as the limits of 'green-revolution' innovations are reached the rate of improvement is slowing significantly, and malnutrition still affects about half a million people in the region. Moreover, with increasing prosperity there is increased demand for foodstuffs such as meat and dairy products, which require more land and water resources. Without advances in genetically modified crops, which some argue pose a greater environmental threat, it is unlikely that the pace of agricultural progress can be sustained. Moreover, many of the pollution problems associated with food production stem from these 'green-revolution' techniques. In fact, agricultural productivity may even decline due to water- and land-quality problems. Agriculture has accounted for the majority of groundwater withdrawal in the region. Seafood from the South China Sea is the main source of protein for 500m people living in its coastal zone, and this number is expected to increase as agricultural productivity plateaus or declines. Overfishing and degradation of marine ecosystems threaten this food supply.

Ecological impacts

Expanding population has led to encroachment on or destruction of ecosystems, notably rainforests in Southeast Asia, and loss of biodiversity. Ecosystems have been further damaged directly by air, soil and water pollution, and indirectly by salinisation and depletion of the water table. The increase in international trade both within the region and with other parts of the globe, along with improvements in transport infrastructure, has led both to increased trade in endangered species and a sharp rise in the number of invasive species competing with or replacing native ones, damaging ecosystems and agriculture. At least 400 invasive species have reached China since 1970, and the cost has been conservatively estimated at $14.5bn annually. Encroachment on ecosystems and intensification of agriculture threaten human health. The number of emerging diseases has quadrupled globally over the last 50 years, principally due to increased population density and expansion of the human population into new environments, and East, Southeast and South Asia contain the worst hot-spots for all categories of emerging diseases. SARS and avian flu are the best-known recent examples.

Natural disasters and resilience

Earthquakes, volcanoes, tsunamis, hurricanes and typhoons, blizzards, floods, droughts and other disasters are a constant background threat in the Asia-Pacific region, which experiences around 80% of global natural disasters. More than 600m people were affected by drought between 1995 and 2004. The 2004 Indian Ocean tsunami caused at least 180,000 deaths and displaced over 1.5m people. Typhoons and flooding in the Bay of Bengal caused at least 300,000 deaths in 1970 and 1974. Environmental degradation can intensify the impact of such disasters: mangrove forests provided significant protection in the 2004 tsunami, and their continued decline will increase the risks for coastal communities. Deforestation contributed to the high death-toll when Cyclone Nargis hit Myanmar in early May 2008. Deforestation and erosion also intensify the risk of land- and mudslides from tectonic activity and flooding.

Environmental security

Besides direct threats to human security and wellbeing, environmental problems can contribute to more traditional national-security threats. Acid rain and other air- and water-pollution problems affect nations beyond those which generate the pollution, and require international solutions. Quarrels over maritime boundaries, exclusive economic zones and overfishing create international tension; the dispute over the Spratly Islands in the South China Sea, involving China, Taiwan, Vietnam, the Philippines and Malaysia, is motivated as much by control of fisheries as it is by potential oil resources. Where major watersheds comprise part of more than one country, such as the Indus (India and Pakistan), Ganges (India and Bangladesh) and Mekong (China, Myanmar, Laos, Thailand, Cambodia and Vietnam) basins, increasing water shortages have the potential to create or increase international tensions. As the use of nuclear power expands in the region, there has been both domestic unrest and international tension over the question of waste disposal. There is also an increased risk of accidental or terrorism-induced release of radioactive material from power plants and fuel-processing facilities. Water and food scarcity can lead to migration, ethnic tensions and political unrest, as can population displacement from dam construction. The aftermath of natural disasters has led to civil unrest in South Asia and China in recent decades.

Global warming and climate change

The latest scientific evidence leaves no doubt that global and regional climates are changing significantly in response to global warming. The Fourth Assessment Report of the UN Intergovernmental Panel on Climate Change (IPCC), issued in 2007, concluded that there was no question that the long-term rise in mean global temperature in the last 250 years was accelerating rapidly, and that the majority of the rise was 'very likely' to be due to increased concentrations of man-made 'greenhouse gases', of which carbon dioxide (CO_2) is the most prominent, if not the most dangerous. South, East and Southeast Asia include three of the top five global emitters of CO_2 (China (2nd), India (4th) and Japan (5th)), and account for about 28% of global emissions, according to the most recent data. Some estimates now make China the world's largest emitter, having surpassed the US within the last year. The impacts of global warming include rising sea levels and population displacement, increasingly severe typhoons and hurricanes, droughts, floods, disruption of water resources, extinctions and other ecological disruptions, wildfires, severe disease outbreaks and declining crop yields and food stocks. In other words, climate change is both an environmental threat and a multiplier, increasing the severity and impact of all the other environmental problems facing the Asia-Pacific region.

Asia's changing climate

Over the course of the last century there have been significant climate changes in Asia. Although global mean surface temperature increased by 0.57–0.96°C between the second half of the nineteenth century and the beginning of the twenty-first, accelerating to a rate of 0.10–0.16°C per decade over the last 50 years, increases in most countries in the region have been higher. Where data are available, measured increases in mean temperature in the twentieth century range from 0.6–1.0°C in coastal areas of Pakistan to 1.0°C in Japan, with decadal rates of increase of 0.1–0.3°C in Southeast Asia and 0.23°C in South Korea. Temperature increases vary seasonally and between climate zones within particular countries.

In Southeast Asia, the frequency and intensity of extreme weather events associated with the cyclical El Niño have increased in the last 20 years, and rainfall has generally decreased. There has been an increase in extreme rains causing flooding in Vietnam and Cambodia, and floods and landslides in the Philippines. The Korean Peninsula and west and south-west China and the Changjiang River have seen increases in precipitation and severe flooding, while northeast and north China have seen decreases. Japan has seen an increase in the annual fluctuation and frequency of extreme rains, with no overall directional trend. India and Pakistan have seen increases in northern areas and decreases in some coastal areas, and Bangladesh has seen decadal anomalies above long-term averages, with serious and recurrent flooding. Many countries in Asia, particularly China and India, have seen significantly longer and more severe heat waves. Rapid melting of glaciers in the Himalaya and Tibetan plateau has caused increased runoff, mudflows and avalanches. The frequency and intensity of Pacific cyclones have increased over recent decades, and there has been an increase in the intensity and a decline in the frequency of cyclones in the Bay of Bengal and Arabian Sea.

Most if not all the environmental stresses experienced in Asian countries in the past few decades – increased water stress and soil degradation, coastal ecosystem damage, drought, desertification, salinisation and forest fires – have thus already been exacerbated by climate change.

Climate projections and impacts
Precise and accurate predictions of future climate are impossible, because they rely on the trajectory of greenhouse-gas emissions, which in turn depend on a large number of political, economic and social variables. However, across a range of assumptions about these variables, the IPCC's temperature projections for the rest of this century suggest a significant acceleration of warming, highest in South and East Asia and at the global average rate in Southeast Asia, with an increase in overall annual precipitation, especially in East Asia. Increases in heat waves, intense precipitation

Key climate-change vulnerabilites in Asia, with confidence assessment

Region	Water	Food	Coastal ecosystems	Health	Land
North Asia	Moderately resilient Medium confidence	Moderately resilient High confidence	Moderately vulnerable Medium confidence	Moderately vulnerable Medium confidence	Moderately vulnerable Medium confidence
Central and West Asia	Highly vulnerable Very high confidence	Highly vulnerable High confidence	Moderately vulnerable Low confidence	Highly vulnerable Medium confidence	Highly vulnerable High confidence
Tibetan Plateau	Moderately vulnerable Medium confidence	Moderately resilient Low confidence	NA	No data	Moderately vulnerable Low confidence
East Asia	Highly vulnerable High confidence	Highly vulnerable Very high confidence	Highly vulnerable High confidence	Moderately vulnerable High confidence	Highly vulnerable High confidence
South Asia	Highly vulnerable High confidence	Highly vulnerable High confidence	Highly vulnerable High confidence	Highly vulnerable Medium confidence	Highly vulnerable High confidence
Southeast Asia	Moderately vulnerable High confidence	Highly vulnerable High confidence	Highly vulnerable High confidence	Highly vulnerable High confidence	Highly vulnerable High confidence

Source: Intergovernmental Panel on Climate Change, Fourth Assessment Report, 2007. ■ = minimum highly vulnerable with high confidence; ■ = minimum moderately vulnerable with high confidence or highly vulnerable with medium confidence; ■ = moderately vulnerable with medium or low confidence.

and cyclone intensity are projected throughout East, South and Southeast Asia.

Seasonal and sub-regional variations in precipitation patterns, however, mean that the projected overall net increase will not necessarily ameliorate problems of water supply and quality. For example, the maximum monthly flow in the Mekong basin is estimated to increase by 35–41% and in the delta by 16–19% over the course of the century, but the minimum monthly flow is estimated to decline by 17–24% and 26–29% in the basin and delta respectively. Overall annual flow will decline by 16–24%. As glaciers melt, there will be an initial increase in seasonal runoff but an eventual overall decline. In all, 500m people in South Asia and 250m Chinese depend on this runoff for their drinking water. The seasonal variation may lead to increased risk of flooding in spring and decreased water supplies in winter. India is projected to reach a state of water stress (where the demand for water temporarily or chronically exceeds available and useable supply) by 2025; in South and Southeast Asia some 120m–1.2bn people are projected to experience increased water stress by the 2020s and 185m–981m by the 2050s.

Rising sea levels will increase the salinisation of coastal groundwater resources, increase the risk of coastal erosion and coastal flooding from storm surges and inundate low-lying areas. In the IPCC's most conservative scenario, the annual number of people affected by coastal flooding will increase by 12–94m, mostly in South Asia, but with substantial numbers in Thailand, Vietnam, Indonesia and the Philippines. One model predicts that more than 2m people will be directly affected by sea-level rise by 2050 in the Brahmaputra and Mekong megadeltas in Bangladesh and Vietnam alone. In Japan, a one-metre rise in sea level could put 4.1m people at risk. Current coastal protection is likely to prove inadequate to cope with the risks.

Overall cereal production in Asia as a whole is likely to decrease substantially by the end of the century. Yields from livestock may decline and aquaculture and fisheries in Asian waters are likely to be adversely affected. One of the IPCC's mid-range projections suggests that, in Asia as a whole, the number of people at risk of hunger could increase by 7–14% by 2020, 14–40% by the 2050s and 14–137%, or up to 266m people, by the 2080s, even without taking into account increased risk of crop pests and weeds and crop and livestock diseases.

Climate change is also expected to exacerbate the risk of vector-borne and water-borne human diseases, and increase morbidity and mortality from heat stress and poor air quality. The risk will increase directly and due to synergies with impacts such as flooding and extreme weather events.

Dealing with the problem
A variety of national and regional structures are in place to respond to Asia's environmental concerns. Most Asian nations have legal and regulatory frameworks to address the problems, but many lack adequate enforcement mechanisms or the technological means for compliance.

- The South Asia Cooperative Environment Programme (SACEP), comprising Afghanistan, Pakistan, India, Sri Lanka, Nepal, Bangladesh and Bhutan, was established in 1982 to promote regional cooperation on the natural and human environment in the context of economic, social and sustainable development and to support the conservation and management of natural resources. It is considered an appropriate forum for action on cross-border environmental issues.
- The Association of Southeast Asian Nations (ASEAN) has established a number of mechanisms, including regular ministerial meetings on the environment (the tenth and most recent was in

2006), a 2002 Agreement on Transboundary Haze Pollution and a Declaration on Environmental Sustainability adopted by the ASEAN heads of state in November 2007, setting out various goals and mechanisms.

- The Northeast Asia Sub-regional Programme for Environment Cooperation (NEASPEC), comprising China, Japan, Mongolia, Russia and North and South Korea, was launched in 1993 as an inter-governmental cooperation mechanism to address regional environmental challenges, with an annual Meeting of Senior Officials on Environmental Cooperation in Northeast Asia.

At the ninth ASEAN+3 (China, Japan and South Korea) summit in Kuala Lumpur in December 2005, heads of government agreed to closer cooperation on issues of sustainable development and the environment. Japan has taken a leadership role with the G8's 2005 3R (Reduce, Reuse and Recycle) initiative, and convened an Asian 3R conference in 2006. These and other organisations provide a framework for addressing regional environmental issues, although most formal cooperation is based on bilateral agreements, success has been variable and serious challenges remain.

Climate change in particular is a global problem and cannot be solved on a regional basis, although regional cooperation on adaptation efforts to deal with environmental and other impacts can be effective. An international regime to mitigate greenhouse-gas emissions and global warming is currently under negotiation through the Bali Roadmap process, which is expected to conclude by the end of 2009. The first session in Bangkok in April 2008 formally launched the process, with the next scheduled for Bonn in June, but there remain serious disagreements between developing and developed countries, particularly Japan and the US, over targets, mechanisms and responsibility. The biggest portion of projected increases in greenhouse gases in the twenty-first century is expected to come from rapidly developing economies such as Indonesia, India and China. These countries, which do not face binding targets under the current Kyoto Protocol (which expires in 2012), take the position that global warming is first and foremost a result of the development of industrialised economies. Despite the fact that India and China are among the world's largest emitters of greenhouse gases in absolute terms, for example, they lag well behind in per-capita emissions. It would be inequitable to force the rest of the world to sacrifice their own development, so there is a moral obligation on the part of the developed world to assist them, financially and technologically, to achieve environmentally sustainable development under the principle of common but differentiated responsibilities. Since the developing countries, particularly in Asia, lag well behind in emissions per unit of gross domestic product (GDP), there is ample scope for such assistance to achieve significant results.

Parallel to the Bali process, under the aegis of the UN Framework Convention on Climate Change, there has also been a series of Major Economies Meetings (MEMs), which include Japan, South Korea, China, Indonesia and India, along with 11 other countries. The fourth such meeting took place in Paris in April. Japan took over chairmanship of the G8 in January 2008, and Japanese Prime Minister Yasuo Fukuda said at the World Economic Forum in Davos that issues concerning the environment and global warming would be at the forefront of the G8 summit in Hokkaido in July. At the same time, Fukuda announced the launch of a $10bn fund to help developing countries cut their emissions. Although a Japanese proposal for structuring emissions targets was rejected at the April Bangkok talks, it will be reconsidered at the Bonn meeting and discussed at Hokkaido. The MEM leaders are also scheduled to meet on the sidelines of the Hokkaido summit to express a 'common shared vision'. These two tracks will in turn feed back into the third Bali process session in August or September.

Principal sources

Intergovernmental Panel on Climate Change, *Climate Change 2007: Impacts, Adaptation and Vulnerability*, Working Group II Contribution to the Fourth Assessment Report of the IPCC (Cambridge: Cambridge University Press, 2007).

United Nations Economic and Social Commission for Asia and the Pacific, *State of the Environment in Asia and the Pacific 2005: Synthesis* (Bangkok: UNESCAP, 2006).

United Nations Environment Programme, *Annual Report 2007* (Nairobi: UNEP, 2008).

United Nations Environment Programme, *Global Environment Outlook 4: Summary for Decision Makers* (Nairobi: UNEP, 2007).

United Nations Environment Programme, Regional Resource Centre for Asia and the Pacific, *Asia-Pacific Environment Outlook 2* (Pathumthani: UNEP RRCAP, 2001).

III: The Widening Security Agenda

Address to the 7th IISS Asia Security Summit,
the Shangri-La Dialogue, Singapore, 1 June 2008

Restoring Peace in Complex Emergencies

Jakob Kellenberger
President, International Committee of the Red Cross

First of all I wish to express the deepest sympathy of the International Committee of the Red Cross (ICRC) to all persons affected by last month's terrible natural disasters in China and Myanmar. My observations today will be related to humanitarian emergencies created both by natural disasters and by armed conflict. I am fully aware that it is the consequences of natural disasters that are your chief concern at present.

On the whole, government agencies and organisations such as the ICRC face similar challenges when they respond to an emergency caused by a natural disaster. Natural disasters (droughts excepted) often occur unexpectedly, and the first hours and days are crucial to saving lives and preventing the spread of epidemics. To minimise the human suffering caused by disaster two things are needed: an assessment of the specific needs of the population and the scale of those needs, and the ability to deliver the required assistance rapidly and efficiently. The main challenge is therefore to become operational as quickly as possible. Capacity for rapid deployment depends on the availability of the proper professional human resources, as well as efficient and flexible logistics. Governments and organisations can prepare themselves to some extent by developing their capacities in both areas. Knowledge of the area, the activation of existing contacts and the ability to build local capacity and skills are all assets.

Governments bear the main responsibility for responding to the needs of their people. In certain cases, because of the scale of the disaster, a variety of other actors might be able or ready to intervene; such opportunities should not be disregarded. When the needs of a population exceed national capacity to respond, government should take advantage of the help offered by international actors. Where governments are reluctant or tardy in accepting assistance on the grounds that they are preserving their sovereignty and want no interference in their domestic affairs, the result may well be many preventable deaths among their people. The attitude of the authorities in countries affected by humanitarian emergencies is therefore crucial.

However, the presence of different actors does create a coordination challenge. To be effective, coordination must be action-oriented and reality-based. To be clear, in situations of emergency, it is not about the coordination of dreams and ambitions, but about existing and available capacities on the ground. Coordination must be built on available human resources, professional capacities and logistical means. I have no doubt at all that an organisation's reputation in the field is determined by its operational capacities, including for rapid deployment. Actions speak louder than words. Humanitarians, like others, must deliver on their promises.

Armed conflicts may flare up unexpectedly, as in Lebanon during the summer of 2006. In such cases, rapid-deployment capacities and the related challenges I have mentioned are relevant. In many cases, there are warning signs, which allow those willing to respond to humanitarian needs to make preparations in advance. Many current conflicts are chronic. The main challenge in responding to humanitarian emergencies created by armed conflict is gaining access to those in need of protection and assistance. Dialogue with all the parties to the conflict is essential to gaining such access. Without dialogue, there can be no guarantee that the humanitarian assistance or those providing it will be accepted.

Clearly, those willing to respond to needs created by natural disasters that occur in a conflict area face all of the aforementioned challenges. Such situations are compounded by the fact that, usually, the authorities will have been weakened by the conflict, as will the public services they deliver, and their capacity to respond to an emergency will be proportionally diminished.

The ICRC is an impartial, neutral and independent organisation whose exclusive humanitarian mission is to protect the lives and dignity of victims of armed conflict and other situations of violence, and to assist them. War is the predominant environment that we work in, and in this context, the ICRC is probably the largest humanitarian actor worldwide, with more than 12,000 staff permanently stationed in the field. The ICRC also endeavours to prevent suffering by promoting and strengthening humanitarian law. Its activities stem from the mandate given to it by the international community, first of all through the Geneva Conventions, which are now ratified by every country in the world. We maintain a presence and are active in 80 countries, where we have around 230 delegations and offices. As a result of this, the organisation has expert knowledge of many very different situations. Today, the ICRC's larger-scale operations are in Sudan, Iraq, Somalia, Afghanistan, Israel and the occupied territories.

The ICRC is also committed to responding to the needs of people affected by natural disasters when they occur in places where the organisation is already operational. Knowledge of the area, appropriate human resources and logistical capacity where they are already in place are crucial to assessing needs in a specific situation and responding to them effectively and rapidly. I believe that we gave convincing proof of our capacity in this regard in the district of Muzaffarabad in Pakistan-administered Kashmir after the earthquake in South Asia in October 2006. This operation also demonstrated the importance of well-coordinated and complementary action, in this case involving the ICRC and the Pakistani armed forces, the main actor in the affected area.

Another instance of the ICRC's intervention in natural disasters was the work done by the organisation following the tsunami of 2004. Some of the stricken areas were affected by ongoing armed conflicts or other situations of violence. The support provided by the Singaporean government and military was rapid and constructive, and it allowed us to establish a professional logistical base in Singapore for our flight operations, in order to organise the delivery of aid. In the natural disaster caused by Cyclone Nargis, the ICRC is supporting the International Federation of Red Cross and Red Crescent Societies and the Myanmar Red Cross Society.

Humanitarian response can be provided by a variety of actors. Methods vary, and there are times when one kind of action is more effective than another, but there should be no confusion between the different actors and their distinctive roles. The ICRC's neutral and independent humanitarian action is always based on dialogue with the concerned parties, and acceptance by them. The organisation's aim is to provide an effective response that will benefit all victims of armed conflicts and violent situations. The ICRC is fully aware that acceptance has to be earned, and can easily be lost, but it is equally convinced that in situations of armed conflict or in sensitive political environments, its neutrality and independence do facilitate access, both to people in need and to the proper authorities. Demonstrating the relevance of this particular approach to humanitarian action is a daily challenge for the ICRC. Our operations in Sudan, Somalia, Afghanistan, Iraq and Sri Lanka, to mention only a few, are convincing examples of the enduring value of neutral and independent humanitarian action.

The main task of national military forces is to ensure the security of their country. But such forces often have a wealth of human resources and logistical capabilities, and experience has shown that their life-saving work in their own countries and in other countries during large-scale natural disasters is irreplaceable. It must be welcomed and encouraged. However, when a humanitarian emergency occurs in an area of conflict, or in a sensitive political context, the situation changes. Armed forces are direct participants in the conflict, or may be perceived as participating in a wider political agenda. In analysing their function from a humanitarian perspective, I will mention three points.

First, in situations where international humanitarian law is applicable, armed forces have the obligation to provide humanitarian assistance to populations under their control, the responsibility that governments have at all times. Second, securing an area is the primary role of any military force, and may have a clear humanitarian dimension, depending on the situation. Indeed, one can only applaud if the civilian population is spared the effects of the fighting by improvements in the security situation. An improved security situation will also facilitate the delivery of public services and humanitarian assistance. Third, when military forces deliver humanitarian assistance themselves, they acquire a more ambiguous role, one which is likely to create conflict with those actors engaged in purely humanitarian missions, and which creates doubts about the independence and neutrality of action. If the prevailing security situation means that no actor other than the military is able to respond to people's needs, lifesaving humanitarian activities carried out by the military can only be welcome. Equally, in my view, military forces should avoid engaging in humanitarian activities if humanitarian actors are able to do the job. In any case, the onus is on them to prove that they are in a better position to undertake such activities than humanitarian actors.

In a complex security environment, effective and timely humanitarian assistance can be delivered only if states – their military forces in particular – and humanitarian actors engage in substantive dialogue and are aware of and respect each other's mandates, principles and modus operandi. Even in the context in which the ICRC is working and its mandate, it is normal that the ICRC is in regular dialogue with military forces all over the world. Afghanistan is a good illustration of the relationship between the ICRC and military actors. The organisation did not participate in civil–military initiatives such as the provincial reconstruction teams, but it is fully committed to discussing a wide range of issues of humanitarian concern, such as the operating procedures for handling detainees captured during the course of hostilities. We see Afghan authorities with US forces, or with commanders from the International Security Assistance Force. This, and other aspects of our dialogue, are indicative of a quality of relationship that is something of a model in civil–military relations, although rather unique. What is important is that such relations have not detracted from the ICRC's ability to maintain its neutrality and independence in Afghanistan, nor has it undermined its ability to develop a dialogue with other armed actors in the same context.

There are other examples of the ICRC's coordination efforts in Asia. The ICRC seeks to interact with regional organisations such the Association of Southeast Asian Nations (ASEAN) Regional Forum and the Shanghai Cooperation Organisation. In order to build a complementary relationship, our organisation aims to establish or intensify dialogue with the political and military authorities that formulate policies for responding to emergencies. In this context, the ICRC's contribution to the drafting of the standard operating procedures of regional mechanisms such as the ASEAN Committee on Disaster Management and its dialogue with the ASEAN Emergency Rapid Assessment Team recently dispatched to Myanmar should be noted. As it is the objective of such mechanisms to strengthen the regional response to emergencies, the ICRC is ready to enter into a wider dialogue and cooperation, including on the subject of the use of neutralised military assets for humanitarian operations.

Address to the IISS Global Strategic Review, Geneva, 14 September 2008

Economics in Conflict Resolution

Ronald Cohen

Chairman, Portland Trust

I would like today to say a few words about what we have been doing at the Portland Trust over the last six years, and share with you the experience and insights that we have gained from trying to address the economic dimension of the Israeli–Palestinian conflict. To explain, the Portland Trust is a British not-for-profit 'action tank' that focuses on the economic dimension of this conflict.

It has been argued that in conflict resolution, addressing economics cannot be a substitute for political action. But, though this is true, after six years of working on this dimension of conflict, it is my view that economics are a necessary condition of conflict resolution. Economics can make peace possible, and can act as a powerful force for moderation. However, the reality is that the priority is often to search for a political solution, then a security solution, and then build institutions, and economics only comes in afterwards. Almost all of the military leaders I have spoken with over the years have said to me that a political agreement must precede any action on the economic front, otherwise it is doomed to failure. My contention is the opposite: that the interdependence of all these different areas with economics is so great that unless you bring the economic dimension to bear at the beginning of the process, you almost doom the process to failure, not to put it too extremely.

The Portland Trust, established in 2003, operates through offices in London, Tel Aviv and Ramallah. On the Palestinian side, we have worked to support Palestinian efforts to develop the private sector. On the Israeli side, we have worked to relieve poverty. Our experience has confirmed the crucial role that economics plays in conflict resolution.

I would like to share with you the example of Northern Ireland, which as a Briton I have been particularly exposed to, because I think it is a powerful illustration of the interdependence of economics and politics. An important lesson from Northern Ireland was that a conflict which had gone on for 300 years and had been marked by 35 years of terrorist violence took a turn for the better when investment started to go into Northern Ireland in 1978. Economic initiatives created incentives to spur political progress. Equality and fairness legislation was introduced and George Mitchell, I will remind you all, was sent by President Bill Clinton in 1993, not as a political envoy, but as an economic envoy. As some momentum began to develop for curbing the terrorist activities of the IRA and for developing and improving the economic situation of the population, so the private sector united and began to speak with a single voice in favour of moderation, through the Northern Irish 'Group of 7', led by Sir George Quigley. The Confederation of British Industry and the Northern Ireland Business Alliance became outspoken opponents of retaliation where violence had taken place. Then US-based firms operating in Northern Ireland introduced the 'MacBride principles' for equal opportunities, and we began to see a move towards an improvement in the employment situation of Catholics in Northern Ireland, which eventually led to very substantial foreign direct investment – between the ceasefire of 1994 and the year 2000, $1.5 billion came in, mainly from the US. Unemployment fell from 17% in 1986 to 4.6% in 2006. We saw some immediate reactions – which can be transferred to the Palestinian example – in jumps in economic activity following the 1994 ceasefire, including in tourism, which increased by 20% in the first year after the ceasefire.

In 1969, Catholic unemployment was around two-and-a-quarter times the level of Protestant unemployment. A very high level of correlation has been found between the ratio of Catholic unemployment to Protestant unemployment and the percentage of Troubles-related deaths caused by Republicans. By 2001, that unemployment ratio had reduced significantly, as had deaths caused by Republicans. Today, unemployment and violence are both low. So we can see the link between unemployment and economic despair and violence.

I would like to turn now to the Middle East, and the Middle East process. I am privileged to have been born in Egypt, which I had to leave at the age of 11 as a result of the Suez Crisis. I have also had a very deep involvement with Israel. Through my old firm Apax Partners, I was involved in introducing the hi-tech venture-capital world to Israel and in more recent years, I have made substantial investments in some of the major companies of Israel.

Between 1994 and 2007, Israel doubled its GDP, from $80bn to $160bn. Palestinian GDP was stuck at $4bn throughout the same period. Israel is not threatened economically; indeed, it would benefit from a thriving Palestinian economy. It is now beginning to permeate Israeli thinking as well as thinking elsewhere that if you could treble the size of the Palestinian economy through growth, which I will try to show can be done, the impact on Israeli growth would be to steepen it. Thus there is a peace dividend for both sides.

Since 1999, there has been nearly a 40% drop in Palestinian real GDP per capita, and a 9% drop in real GDP in the same period. Yet if you look at the Palestinian economy, it is diverse, with half a dozen very powerful sectors, which I will come to in a moment. Palestine has a highly literate, entrepreneurial population with a 97% literacy rate (the rate in Egypt is 57%). In terms of population – 3.8 million – and literacy rates, Palestine is almost identical to Lebanon, which has three times its GDP. This is an economy that has attracted very considerable amounts of aid – $2bn per year. International aid was 35% of Palestinian GDP in 2006 and 50% of GDP in 2007. If you look at the cost to the international community of paying $2bn per year and transform it into a capital sum, what is the sum that you would need to invest today to be able to provide $2bn or so indefinitely? Fifty billion dollars. Thus, capital expended to sort out this conflict would more than pay for itself.

My contention is that the Palestinian economy could be three times its current size. It could grow at more than 10% a year. Prime Minister Salam Fayyad, with whom I have had the privilege to work over the last few years, is an intelligent, sophisticated, moderate person, capable of leading Palestinians towards this much larger economy. But this expansion can only be achieved through the development of the private sector, and one of the key conclusions of our work is that the emphasis on developing public-sector expenditure is to a large degree a problem in the making. You can still see it in Northern Ireland, where the British government continues to invest £8bn a year in budgetary support. In order to get a sustainable economic life for the populations of these countries marked by conflict, we must put great emphasis on developing the private sector.

There are six well-defined sectors in the Palestinian economy: agriculture; finance; information and communication technology; infrastructure and construction; manufacturing; and tourism. The construction industry in particular is an important sector. In May, I spoke at the Palestine Investment Conference in Bethlehem. Israel was extremely cooperative in allowing access to the conference and extremely helpful in its organisation. More than 1,200 people attended, from the Gulf, Middle Eastern and Western countries, and $1.4bn of investment was announced. Prime Minister Fayyad made it clear that as far as he was concerned, Palestine is now open for business.

So what does Palestinian private-sector development involve? I would like to give you a microeconomic view of what needs to be done. If I were to say to you that there were 22 banks operating in the Palestinian territories, you might be surprised. Equally, if I said to you that these banks only invest 20% of the deposits they gather back into the area, you might well be shocked. The reason for this, of course, is that the risk profile of investment in Palestine today is extremely high. In order, therefore, to get the banks back to work, Fayyad and UK Prime Minister Gordon Brown (who was Chancellor of the Exchequer when the project began) have developed a scheme for loan guarantees to the private sector to fund small- and medium-enterprise expansion, a scheme which the Portland Trust helped to design, with the help of the Aspen Institute. Both the Overseas Private Investment Corporation in the US and the European Investment Bank now operate in Palestine with $200m of guarantees. If a bad loan is made, 70% of the loss stays with the guarantors and 30% with the banks.

We have also worked on the area of microfinance, and support for the microfinance network and training. But while microfinance helps with self-employment, in order to have a sustainable economy, you need to build significantly sized businesses, and there is virtually no source of long-term capital formation in Palestine. To take an example, private-sector pension funds in Palestine only contain $60m. In response to this, we have been working with Prime Minister Fayyad and his colleagues to design a modern private-sector pensions scheme to provide long-term capital accumulation, which we hope will be introduced at the beginning of next year.

Affordable housing is a particularly important project that we have been addressing. There are clearly challenges connected to the movement of people and goods in this region – Israel is interested in giving maximum movement to Palestinians, but at the same time, Israel's government is very sensitive to the risk of a terror attack. So, as one looks through the various possible avenues for providing a big boost to the Palestinian economy, almost by a process of elimination, one inevitably lights on construction. The Portland Trust has been working through the private sector on a billion-dollar investment programme to support Palestinian entrepreneurs who own land and are interested in developing new communities in building 15,000 homes in six new communities on the West Bank. Our activities are at the moment confined to the West Bank, as we are following the policy of the British government in not currently dealing with Gaza. We expect the project to bring thousands of new jobs and improve the lives of over 200,000 Palestinians, and lead to an increase in Palestinian GDP of 1.5% a year over five years. The important insight here is that most of the money for the project can come from the private sector – it does not need to be funded through grants alone.

Leveraging donor funding through private-sector investment is, in my view, the most effective way to boost the development of the private sector in situations such as these. In working to achieve a stronger private sector, the most effective role for donors is to improve the risk–return profile, so as to attract private-sector capital. This particular programme is an excellent example of how donor funding can attract private investment. The billion-dollar investment breaks down as follows. There is the layer of grant from donors, to fund infrastructure and public facilities. We suggest that, in the case of this project and perhaps in that of many others, this layer should be around 15%, or $150m. Then one can leverage in $100m for the value of the land on which the projects are going to be built. Another $100m would be the 10% deposits that the purchasers of the apartments would put down on their mortgages, and a further $650m would be covered by 15-year fixed mortgages on the properties.

To give you an insight into what is involved in getting something like this going, if a Palestinian entrepreneur tried to build even 5,000 homes without the help of the international community, people would think he had gone mad. The reason for this is that a very substantial upfront investment is needed – in infrastructure, roads, sewage, electricity, water – and he would not know if Israel would support the building work. If such an entrepreneur had gone to Palestinian banks for finance a year ago, all that he could have got would have been five years' worth of funding at variable rates of interest, which would have made him feel extremely insecure.

So the role of the international community in situations such as these is an enabling one. It has the ability to bring together the different parties that are involved in making a project of this kind possible. In this case, we hope that the first $400m of this investment, to build 5,000 homes, will begin at the turn of the year, and Qatar has invested as an equity investor in the scheme.

In my view, as a general rule, grants that leverage in private-sector financing are the most effective way of developing the private sector. If, for the sake of argument, it were possible to acquire $1bn-worth of grants from the World Bank or similar organisations, I believe that up to $6bn could be attracted in private-sector equity and debt for projects. The effect of such an investment would be that Palestinian GDP would grow at a rate of 10.5% a year for five years. In addition to housing, sectors that might benefit from this approach include infrastructure and construction, agriculture, energy, health and other areas.

The difficulty today is that people like my colleagues and I at the Portland Trust cannot go to a single address such as the World Bank in order to raise this grant finance. We must approach the British government, the Italian government, other governments, the EU, and try to persuade these states and the EU to provide money on an ad hoc basis for a private-sector project. Very often there is a reluctance on the part of international aid organisations within nations to provide help directly to the private sector. There is a fear that somehow this will help individuals to enrich themselves and that this will become a focus for criticism. Yet if you want to create moderation in a society, you do it not by channelling your investment through governments, but by channelling it directly to the private sector.

What might the principles be on which institutions such as those that I have mentioned could make this sort of funding available? Obviously, an initial focus on large investment projects will have more impact. Projects to focus on are those that generate growth, create jobs, improve living standards and bring in additional tax revenues to the Palestinian Authority, but which cannot proceed on a commercial basis without the grant. We would suggest a grant layer of 15% of the project, to reduce risk and increase equity return to a commercial level. Fifteen per cent transforms the risk–return proposition for all those involved in investing. The grant should be approved at the start of the project, in order to attract equity and debt. All too often – and I know that ex-Prime Minister Tony Blair has been struggling with this – donor states require a project to be complete before they will provide a grant. This is putting the cart before the horse. Those of you involved in the business world will know the difficulties if you are not able to say to potential investors and bankers that you have a grant at a particular level, at 15%, that the project is functioning. One can end up going round in circles, with people asking to see the next layer of funding before they will offer funding themselves.

Conditions need to be attached to the grant. This is an important principle for ensuring long-term outcomes. In the case of the project I described earlier, those outcomes would be the affordability of the housing, a level of pricing at which Palestinians will be able to purchase their apartments; access to the development, access by the population to the finance required for the development; and the sustainability of the project. Access and sustainability are crucial, because the aim is to build a thriving economy and then release the grant as the equity is invested.

Finally, it is necessary to ring-fence the grant facility to prevent diversion to the general government budget. Clearly, the general budget will always be the top priority of a government in a conflict situation, and unless you segregate this money, the private sector will get very little of the investment that has been allocated.

In conclusion, after six years of work on the Israeli–Palestinian conflict, it is our view that the economic dimension is essential to resolving this conflict. Only with the prospect of ongoing prosperity can a political solution be reached and become a long-lasting peace. Private-sector development is vital, not only to sustainable economic growth, but also to act as a force for moderation. In conflict and post-conflict situations, the government and the international community must support the development of the private sector and encourage investment and economic progress. Foreign direct investment is a crucial element in helping conflict situations emerge into sustainable societies. One of the most effective ways to stimulate the private sector is to leverage in private-sector finance through the establishment of a leveraging grant facility. This, and other actions to support the economy, must come at the beginning of the conflict-resolution process, alongside the politics, security and institution-building with which it is interdependent.

Dinner Address to the IISS–AIPS Korea Forum, 26 September 2008

Assessing Political Risk

Nigel Inkster

Director of Transnational Threats and Political Risk, IISS

I would like to begin with a reflection on the Day of Judgement as seen through the eyes of my Scottish Calvinist forebears, a stern, unforgiving people whose philosophy of life can best be summed up by the proposition that 'we were not put on this earth to enjoy ourselves'. The story goes that on the Day of Judgement all mankind was brought before the Archangel Gabriel to face an assessment of their conduct while on Earth. The many who were judged to have been irredeemable sinners were condemned to spend all eternity suffering the torments of Hell. As the sinners were waiting to be cast down into the everlasting fires, they looked up and saw the face of the Lord and cried out in piteous tones, 'Lord, Lord, we didna ken, we didna ken' – for those of you unfamiliar with Scottish dialect, that means 'We didn't know, we didn't know.' And the Lord, in his infinite wisdom and mercy, looked down upon the faces of the poor sinners and said 'Yes, well, you know now.' And that I think is a good starting point for a talk on assessing political risk. Ignorance really is no excuse.

Over the past decade we have witnessed, at least in the Anglo-Saxon world, a massive upsurge in what might be termed the 'risk industry'. And here I'm talking about risk in the widest and most generic sense, defined as the probability of something going wrong multiplied by the impact of its doing so. Risk assessment and risk management are now supposed to be at the heart of corporate management culture, with 'risk registers' and directors responsible for risk. Much of this approach has been driven by the fallout from major financial scandals such as Enron. But if the recent developments in the US financial sector are anything to go by, it would seem that the risk-based management system is still in need of some refinement. The reality is in fact simpler and more banal. What seems to have happened is that directors of companies in the financial sector simply did not and could not understand the risks their companies were running, despite being legally liable for these risks. It seems clear that if the financial crisis ever settles down, more thought will need to be given to how a system more fit for purpose can be developed. But – perhaps fortunately – that is beyond the scope of this evening's talk.

The topic this evening is political risk. What do we mean by that? The classic definition is probably that given by Professor Louis T. Wells of the Harvard Business School: 'threats to profitability that are external to the business and which arise from government action or inaction'. That definition still holds good, but it may not encompass the way in which political risk has developed since Wells produced it. Since the 1980s, a sea change in the global economy, in which developing nations moved away from autarky and a focus on import substitution to a policy of actively courting foreign direct investment, combined with declining business opportunities in the developed world, has driven many Western companies to move into emerging markets, with accompanying levels of risk much greater than those to which many had been accustomed. Those companies which moved into emerging markets on the presumption that business was business the world over quickly came to grief. *Mr China*, a book written by British investment banker Tim Clissold, depicts in graphic terms what can and did go wrong when insufficient account was taken of local political and cultural factors. Since the early days, an approach to political risk which could often be described as pro forma has now become focused and serious – and supported by a huge industry specialising in different aspects of political-risk analysis.

Traditionally, political risk has been seen in terms of government risk and instability risk; in essence, the risk either that the government of a particular country might expropriate one's assets, or that a country might suffer a level of internal instability – insurgency or even civil war – which makes the conduct of normal business either difficult or impossible. From the 1950s through to the 1970s, the risk of expropriation was very real, as numerous newly independent nations, often following socialist models of development, sought to acquire control of what were then deemed strategic assets. Latterly, this concern has been less salient, although recent developments in countries such as Venezuela, Bolivia and Russia suggest that economic nationalism may be about to make a comeback, a process which might be exacerbated if, as seems increasingly likely, the global economy suffers a prolonged slowdown.

The globalisation of markets has led to the globalisation of political risk. This has a number of important consequences. Among these is the degree to which organisations that might normally be risk averse and disinclined to venture overseas looking for new business increasingly find that risk comes to them even if they do not go to it. A banker might, for example, decide not to open a branch office in Russia. But if a high-value Russian client shows up wanting to open an account, the bank in question is brought face-to-face with Russian political risk. In this regard, the global preponderance of the US has had a significant impact, as a result of both extraterritoriality and international sanctions. This has been evidenced by the extensive application of, respectively, the Foreign Corrupt Practices Act, and the Iran–Libya Sanctions Act and Iran Proliferation Act. Two years ago, the US arm of a Dutch bank was compelled to pay an $80 million fine for failing to make adequate arrangements to ensure compliance with the Iran–Libya Act.

The final category of political risk to which I would like briefly to refer is reputational, and it is here that international civil society, in particular in the form of non-governmental organisations, plays a major role. Anyone who has ever run an organisation will be acutely aware of how fragile reputation can be and how easy it is for one remark or one action to cancel out years of high-quality performance. Examples are legion of specific organisations suffering reputation damage due to the way in which third parties, particularly NGOs, have taken up, publicised and campaigned against particular behaviours or activities. De Beers and conflict diamonds, Shell and BP in Colombia and Shell and Exxon in Nigeria are some of the better-known examples. The point to note is that although the risk arises in the country of operation, it increasingly manifests itself transnationally, in a virtual arena where the normal rules do not apply. Most companies now, when confronting investment decisions, will as a matter of course ask where the NGOs stand on that investment and consider how to manage and mitigate their responses.

So if political risk matters, how are we to measure and assess it so as to minimise the risk of unexpected shock and unwelcome surprises and optimise our chances of coming out ahead? There are some kinds of risk that lend themselves to quantitative analysis. These risks tend to be the kind that can be defined numerically and which fall within predictable ranges. The insurance industry makes extensive use of such models, as do the major hedge funds, whose quantitative-analysis models seem, for the time being at least, to bring them out ahead of the markets. But I suspect that these models may have their limitations, and that they are unlikely to be able to deal with 'black swans' – an analogy developed by the US writer Nassim Nicholas Taleb to describe events so far removed from the realm of previous experience as to give rise to a paradigm shift. It is important to remember that these models are developed by people with similar backgrounds, similar levels of knowledge and similar sets of assumptions. In situations where those assumptions do not apply, there has to be some risk that they can represent a kind of electronic groupthink, a GPS system for guiding the lemmings over the cliff. So it is important to bear in mind their limitations.

I know that there are many political-risk experts and organisations who claim that it is possible to apply at least some aspects of quantitative analysis to political risk. I cannot disprove these assertions. But I am profoundly sceptical, and so as an institution is the IISS. I can well understand why people in the business community crave the certainty of hard figures. But if asked to give a percentage probability that, say, the US will attack Iran in the next two years, I find it impossible to offer a convincing response. Sixty per cent? Then why not 59% or 61%? And is the provision of such a figure not actively counterproductive if it provides false comfort and prevents people from thinking about the nuances of the issue?

In general, I believe that political risk is better approached using qualitative models, such as the scenario-planning approach pioneered by Shell. This approach posits a range of potential outcomes for particular situations, in order both to make judgements about which are most likely and to enable decision-makers to consider possible responses to a range of different eventualities. The scenarios are illustrative, and do not purport to predict the future. There are of course many snake-oil merchants who seek to persuade us that they can develop systems which will predict the future, if only we pay them enough. My strong recommendation is that if you are faced with such a person, reach for your revolver.

Because when it comes to predicting the future, the picture is quite clear. We simply cannot do it. There are too many variables and too many possible combinations, in addition to the uncertainties that arise from the vagaries of human behaviour. The record of the human race in this regard ought to speak for itself. But if that is not sufficiently convincing, there is a body of scientific evidence deriving from detailed experiments which demonstrate the point. There is a book that I would recommend to any of you interested in this topic: *Expert Political Judgement: How Good is It? How Can We Know?*, by Canadian academic Philip Tetlock. It is an excellent read, and its conclusions are compelling and accessible. As a species, we are startlingly bad at predicting the future. But there are some people who consistently achieve better results than the average, albeit with low overall percentages, typically in the twenties and low thirties. That is the good news. The bad news is that these are, in the main, not the sorts of people who tend to become senior decision-makers. They are cautious, pragmatic people whose instinct is to weigh the evidence carefully and not leap to premature conclusions. In the analogy popularised by Sir Isaiah Berlin, they are foxes, people who know lots of little things and who build pragmatic models to help them make sense of the information they have, rather than hedgehogs, people who know one big thing and tend to look for evidence which supports that. In a word, the first set of people are not well-suited to the sound-bite world we live in. But to the extent that their voices can be heard, the quality of political-risk analysis is likely to be better than it might otherwise be.

There are some traps that we ought to be able to avoid so that, if we do not make good judgements, we at least avoid making seriously bad ones. The key pitfalls are:

- Persuading ourselves that some things will not happen, even though they could. As a species, we are remarkably good at this. We are also remarkably susceptible to all the Great Lies. You know the kind – 'the cheque is in the mail' is a popular one. In terms of political-risk analysis, the most terrifying of all has to be 'this time, it will be different'. How many times did I hear that said about Iraq in the latter part of 2002? And about the British economy over the past decade?

- Making assumptions that other actors will share our values and desire the same outcomes as ourselves, a common flaw among Western politicians who struggle to put themselves into the mindset of leaders from radically different cultures. Again, Iraq demonstrates the dangers. We all thought Saddam Hussein had lost the First Gulf War. Saddam thought he had won it. We all thought Saddam would be afraid of a US invasion. Saddam was much more worried about losing the respect of his immediate neighbours, and did not take the US threat seriously. We all thought that when the invasion began, Saddam would blow the bridges across the Euphrates to stall the American advance. Saddam needed those bridges to move his troops south to suppress Shia rebellions, a much more pressing preoccupation than an American invasion. And so on.

The general conclusion I would draw is that in attempting to assess risk, the factors most likely to make for success are:

- A pragmatic, open-minded approach, avoiding ideology or dogma, considering dissenting views and what a former boss of mine called 'inconvenient information', and showing readiness to learn from mistakes.
- An integrated approach. Risk assessment, like security – with which there is much overlap – works best when it becomes part of the corporate culture and is seen as integral to planning processes, rather than something retrofitted to a 'pure' business plan.
- Avoidance of any approach that seeks to automate risk analysis to the point where decision-makers are left feeling that this is an issue they do not own and do not need to spend time on.

To sum up, I do not believe that there is or ever can be a holy grail for assessing political risk, no single methodology so manifestly superior to all the others that it becomes the industry standard. But equally, in today's world, we cannot afford to be indifferent to the wider environment in which we operate, and globalisation has made that environment infinitely more complex than it was before. As Tolstoy put it in the opening lines of *Anna Karenina*, 'Happy families are all happy in the same way. Unhappy families are each unhappy in their own way.' Achieving happiness involves identifying and avoiding multiple sources of risk, and failure results in unhappiness, the nature of which is defined by the risk that is not avoided. By applying the kind of approach outlined above, we can at least give ourselves some prospect of achieving happiness. But we should also accept that there can be no system which will guarantee it.

IISS
ADELPHI PAPERS

ADELPHI PAPER 399

Joining al-Qaeda: Jihadist Recruitment in Europe

Peter R. Neumann

ISBN 978-0-415-54731-4

ADELPHI PAPER 398

The Iranian Nuclear Crisis: Avoiding worst-case outcomes

Mark Fitzpatrick

ISBN 978-0-415-46654-7

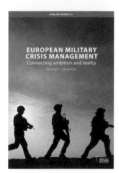

ADELPHI PAPER 397

European Military Crisis Management: Connecting ambition and reality

Bastian Giegerich

ISBN 978-0-415-49419-9

ADELPHI PAPER 396

Abolishing Nuclear Weapons

George Perkovich and James M. Acton

ISBN 978-0-415-46583-0

ADELPHI PAPER 395

Selective Security: War and the United Nations Security Council since 1945

Adam Roberts and Dominik Zaum

ISBN 978-0-415-47472-6

ADELPHI PAPER 394

Ending Terrorism: Lessons for defeating al-Qaeda

Audrey Kurth Cronin

ISBN 978-0-415-45062-1

For credit card orders call **+44 (0) 1264 343 071** or e-mail **book.orders@tandf.co.uk**

Routledge
Taylor & Francis Group

The Evolution of Strategic Thought
Classic Adelphi Papers

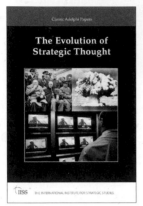

The Adelphi Papers monograph series is the Institute's principal contribution to policy-relevant, original academic research. Collected on the occasion of the Institute's 50th anniversary, the twelve Adelphi Papers in this volume represent some of the finest examples of writing on strategic issues. They offer insights into the changing security landscape of the past half-century and glimpses of some of the most significant security events and trends of our times, from the Cold War nuclear arms race, through the oil crisis of 1973, to the contemporary challenge of asymmetric war in Iraq and Afghanistan.

Published April 2008; 704 pp.

CONTENTS:

Introduction
Patrick M. Cronin

The Evolution of NATO
Adelphi Paper 1, 1961
Alastair Buchan

Controlled Response and Strategic Warfare
Adelphi Paper 19, 1965
T. C. Schelling

The Control of Proliferation: Three Views
Adelphi Paper 29, 1966
Solly Zuckerman, Alva Myrdal and Lester B. Pearson

Israel and the Arab World: The Crisis of 1967
Adelphi Paper 41, 1967
Michael Howard and Robert Hunter

The Asian Balance of Power: A Comparison with European Precedents
Adelphi Paper 44, 1968
Coral Bell

Change and Security in Europe: Part II: In Search of a System
Adelphi Paper 49, 1968
Pierre Hassner

Urban Guerrilla Warfare
Adelphi Paper 79, 1971
Robert Moss

Oil and Influence: The Oil Weapon Examined
Adelphi Paper 117, 1975
Hanns Maull

The Spread of Nuclear Weapons: More May Be Better
Adelphi Paper 171, 1981
Kenneth N. Waltz

Intervention and Regional Security
Adelphi Paper 196, 1985
Neil Macfarlane

Humanitarian Action in War: Aid, Protection and Impartiality in a Policy Vacuum
Adelphi Paper 305, 1996
Adam Roberts

The Transformation of Strategic Affairs
Adelphi Paper 379, 2006
Lawrence Freedman

Bookpoint Ltd. 130 Milton Park, Abingdon, Oxon OX14 4SB, UK
Tel: +44 (0)1235 400524, Fax: +44 (0)1235 400525
Customer orders: book.orders@tandf.co.uk
Bookshops, wholesalers and agents:
Email (UK): uktrade@tandf.co.uk,
email (international): international@tandf.co.uk

Routledge
Taylor & Francis Group

THE INTERNATIONAL INSTITUTE FOR STRATEGIC STUDIES

PERSPECTIVES ON
INTERNATIONAL SECURITY
Speeches and Papers from the
50th Anniversary Year of the
International Institute for Strategic Studies

EDITED BY

TIM HUXLEY AND ALEXANDER NICOLL

ADELPHI PAPER 400–401

The International Institute for Strategic Studies

Arundel House | 13–15 Arundel Street | Temple Place | London | WC2R 3DX | UK

ADELPHI PAPER 400–401

First published December 2008 by **Routledge**
4 Park Square, Milton Park, Abingdon, Oxon, OX14 4RN

for **The International Institute for Strategic Studies**
Arundel House, 13–15 Arundel Street, Temple Place, London, WC2R 3DX, UK
www.iiss.org

Simultaneously published in the USA and Canada by **Routledge**
270 Madison Ave., New York, NY 10016

Routledge is an imprint of Taylor & Francis, an Informa Business

DIRECTOR-GENERAL AND CHIEF EXECUTIVE John Chipman
EDITOR Tim Huxley
MANAGER FOR EDITORIAL SERVICES Ayse Abdullah
ASSISTANT EDITOR Katharine Fletcher
PRODUCTION John Buck
COVER IMAGES (From top, l–r) Lee Hsien Loong (IISS); German soldiers
arrive in DR Congo (Maurizio Gambarini/DPA/PA); Robert Gates (IISS);
Carl Bildt (IISS); US soldiers in Iraq (Daniel Herrera/US Army); Ma Xiaotian
(IISS); Shanghai Pudong office towers (iStockphoto.com/Frank Leung); Karl
Eikenberry (IISS); Amazon deforestation (iStockphoto.com/Joseph Luoman)

Printed and bound in Great Britain by Bell & Bain Ltd, Thornliebank, Glasgow

British Library Cataloguing in Publication Data
A catalogue record for this book is available from the British Library

Library of Congress Cataloging in Publication Data
A catalogue record for this book is available from the Library of Congress

ISBN 978-0-415-54732-1
ISSN 0567-932X